Linlithgow
OLD AND NEW

Spring colour in Blackness Road with the faint silhouettes of St. Michael's Church and Linlithgow Palace in the background.

Edited by Ronald Smith

Linlithgow Civic Trust

List of Sponsors and Subscribers

The Civic Trust is very grateful to all the organisations, companies and individuals who provided financial sponsorship and advance payment towards the costs of the production of this book. Without the help of those listed below, publication would not have been possible.

Main Sponsors

EB Scotland Ltd, Glasgow.
West Lothian Council, Libraries.

Corporate and Private Sponsors

Jack and Christine Adair, Hillside, Linlithgow.
Mr and Mrs P Bailey, Camuscross, Isle of Skye.
Janette Nixon, Clarendon Crescent, Linlithgow.
The Pollock Hammond Partnership, Architects, Grange West, Linlithgow.
Fiona Sinclair, Gatehead, Formakin, Renfrewshire.
Alan Steel Asset Management Ltd, Nobel House, Linlithgow.
West Lothian Council Libraries: Local History Library, Blackburn.
West Lothian Council Libraries: School Resource Service, Blackburn.

Subscribers

June and Alex Adam, Linlithgow.
Mr and Mrs J Alford, Glenrothes, Fife.
Gordon and Liz Beetham, Laverock Park, Linlithgow.
Chris Beetham, Ashtead, Surrey.
Paul Beetham, Little Sandhurst, Berkshire.
E L Burrows, Strawberry Bank, Linlithgow.
Mr and Mrs William Cadell, Linlithgow.
Douglas and Norma Culross, Thornyhall, Dalkeith.
John and Jean Davidson, Friars Way, Linlithgow.
John Dolby, Hull, East Yorkshire.
Mrs Margaret Douglas, Glenrothes, Fife.
Mr and Mrs A S Downs, Griffiths Street, Falkirk.
Dave du Feu, Greenpark Cottages, Linlithgow.
Mike Fraser, Craigmore View, Aberfoyle.
Colin and Joy Galloway, Oatlands Park, Linlithgow.
Janet and David Horner, Copmanthorpe, York.
Cathie and Neil Irvine, St. Magdalene's, Linlithgow.
Mr and Mrs Bruce Jamieson, Baronshill Avenue, Linlithgow.
Brian A G Jenkins-Doig, Leven, Fife.
Mrs Myra K Keir, Lawside, Dundee.
Myra and John Lawson, Linlithgow.
Linlithgowshire Journal and Gazette, Linlithgow.
David Long, Friars Way, Linlithgow.

Jim and Nuala Lonie, Canal House, Linlithgow.
David and Judi Mackie, Mannerston Holdings, Blackness.
Lewis MacSween, Nutberry Court, Glasgow.
Alan and Alison Miller, Royal Terrace, Linlithgow.
Alan and Catherine Moodie, Bonnytoun House, Linlithgow.
Ronald Myles, Linlithgow.
Miss Margaret Morrison, Royal Terrace, Linlithgow.
Mr and Mrs C Neil, Hillhouse, Linlithgow.
Bill Nicol, Jock's Hill Crescent, Linlithgow.
Iain Paterson, Lednock Road, Stepps.
Rev J L Paterson and Mrs L Paterson, St Michael's Manse, Linlithgow.
William and Elizabeth Ross, Friars Brae, Linlithgow.
A and M Shelton, Sheriffs Park, Linlithgow.
Calum Smith, Rivaldsgreen Crescent, Linlithgow.
Flora Smith, Rivaldsgreen Crescent, Linlithgow.
Mrs Lorna Smith, Methil, Fife.
Mike and Catherine Smith, Baronshill Avenue, Linlithgow.
Jess and Ian Stirling, Douglas Cottage, Linlithgow.
Carol and Jim Thomson, Rivaldsgreen Crescent, Linlithgow.
Mr and Mrs J N Tierney, Rivaldsgreen Crescent, Linlithgow.
Julia C Wade, Fairway, Linlithgow.
Alan and Margaret Young, Springfield Road, Linlithgow.

Preface

The Rt Hon Tam Dalyell MP

In this day and age, to address someone as a 'Black Bitch' can lead to all sorts of unfortunate misunderstandings! For those who do not know the folklore of Linlithgow, such language might be deemed offensive – on grounds of gender, good manners and respect for others – let alone political correctitude.

Yet, those of us, men no less than women, who have ancestors born and bred within the Marches, extending to the medieval port of Blackness, respect the she-dog under the oak tree, which barked at the right moment at a time of peril in the 14th century, and which adorns the burgh's coat of arms.

Linlithgow, greatly enhanced by incomers, albeit not Black Bitches, in the second half of the 20th century, has a rich past. Whenever there was disease in Edinburgh, or, indeed, when it came to the time for the "sweetening or airing of the palaces at Holyrood", at the mercy of the stench of the capital, the royal court would decamp to Linlithgow.

We were then more than a halfway house to Stirling! From the medieval tanneries, through high-quality paper-making for the *Illustrated London News* of the 19th and early 20th century, to the state-of-the-art electronics of today, Linlithgow has a rich industrial history too.

This is why, as a Freeman of West Lothian, and a Black Bitch, I salute the work of Linlithgow Civic Trust, only one of whose many contributions to the preservation of the history is this excellent volume, 'Linlithgow Old and New'.

House of Commons,
5 July 2002.

Contents

1	The Royal Burgh of Linlithgow	4
2	Historical Introduction	5
3	Palace, Church and Loch	20
4	Around the Cross	28
5	East High Street	34
6	High and Low Ports	40
7	The Eastern Fringes	44
8	Around the Canal and Railway Station	50
9	The Southern Suburbs	56
10	The Vennel	62
11	West of the Sheriff Court	68
12	West High Street	72
13	Around the West Port	78
14	South West Linlithgow	86
15	Linlithgow Bridge	92
16	Local Customs and Events	96
	References and Photographic Credits	101
	Street Plan of Linlithgow	102
	Index	104

Below The two sides of the common seal of the Royal Burgh of Linlithgow. One side shows the Archangel Michael with wings outstretched, standing on the belly of a serpent and holding a shield decorated with the Royal Arms of Scotland, while the reverse shows a greyhound bitch chained to an oak tree. The current seal can be traced back to at least 1673, but its origins are probably far more ancient.

1

The Royal Burgh of Linlithgow

Linlithgow is a historic town, strategically located in Scotland's central belt, a little east of midway between the great cities of Edinburgh and Glasgow. Dramatically situated between the loch and rising ground to the south, the town was first mentioned in a charter of 1138 and created a Royal Burgh in 1389. Its royal palace ensured prominence for the town in Scottish history, and, by the 15th and 16th centuries, Linlithgow had reached its period of greatest influence, prosperity and architectural achievement. The Union of the Crowns in 1603, together with the loss of the town's coastal trading monopoly through Blackness, caused a decline to relative insignificance, other than its role as the County Town of Linlithgowshire or West Lothian.

The town's original, typically Scottish, linear burgh layout has been largely preserved, partly because of the barriers created by the east-west Union Canal and railway on the steep slopes to the south. Linlithgow is now a popular dormitory town with electronics as its main industry, and, in 1994, it was named 'Scottish Tourism Town of the Year'. Such is its popularity as a place to live, the population has increased from 4,570 in 1951 to 12,500 in 1995.

The town signboard in Falkirk Road, showing the heraldic symbols on the burgh seal in the form of shields - Linlithgow is unusual therefore in having two 'coats of arms'. Also shown on the board is one of the town's two popular mottos: "My Fruit is Fidelity to God and the Queen". The other, as displayed on St. Michael's Well at the east end of the High Street, is "St. Michael is kinde to straingers".

2

Historical Introduction

Linlithgow has been visited over the centuries by calamities which wreaked havoc on the fabric of the burgh. At the end of the 13th century, Edward I descended on it with unfriendly intent; in 1337, the English army set fire to the town; there were further fires in the early 15th century; in 1650, Cromwell's army recycled the buildings of the Kirkgate into new fortifications around the palace; three centuries later, the planning authorities were allowed to demolish large chunks of the High Street.

Origins

It is commonly stated that Linlithgow dates back to the 12th century and was founded by King David I. This has more to do with an improvement in the feudal records of the early 1100s than to a sudden outburst of building in the area. What emerges through the narrow view of David I's charters is that, at the beginning of the 12th century, there was a place called Linlithgow, with a mansion, a church, and burgh status. None of this could have happened overnight, and in all probability, Linlithgow had already existed for some time. The gravel promontory, overlooking the loch in the valley between the Bathgate Hills and Airngath Hill, was an enticing site for kings to establish a dominating presence. There may well have been earlier unrecorded settlements.

In 1136, the approximate date of the earliest surviving charter relating to Linlithgow, the whole area was in the King's lordship. He gave to the newly founded Augustinian Priory of St Andrews the church of Linlithgow with its chapels and lands, both within and outwith the burgh. There was therefore already an established burghal and religious structure.

In a charter of the same period, King David gave to his newly founded Abbey of Holyrood "all the skins of the rams, sheep and lambs from the castle and from Linlitcu which will die in my lordship". There were gifts a few years later of burgh tofts and of the lands of Kettilstoun to the Abbey of Cambuskenneth. The Latin text of this early charter is ambiguous, and this has led to historical misunderstandings: the castle referred to is not that of Linlithgow, as is usually assumed. Later confirming charters of Holyrood Abbey are more precise and replace 'castle' with 'castle of the maidens' (Edinburgh Castle). There was undoubtedly a royal residence at Linlithgow in the early 12th century, but no evidence that it was ever a castle. Malcolm IV and William the Lion are known to have lived there occasionally, but it was not used as a stronghold. In the late 13th century, the residence is referred to in French as *manoir* and in Latin as either *manerium* or *mansum*, which all suggest a lord's house, a manor, with some land, probably built of wood, certainly not a fortified structure. 14th-century English records also refer to the 'King's house' or 'manor'.

In 1187, Pope Gregory VIII confirmed the gift to the Priory of St Andrews of the church of Linlithgow, which by then included the school and the teinds (tithes) of the parish, so that by the reign of William the Lion, we know that there was already a school in the town.

The likely scenario is that the royal residence had prompted the development of a settlement to service it, rather than an existing settlement giving rise to a royal house, for most significant towns would normally develop along major rivers. The settlement already included the building on the promontory, the church next to it, the Kirkgate and probably the High Street, a medieval layout which partly survives. In 1242, the church of Linlithgow was consecrated by David de Bernham, Bishop of St Andrews, but this may have been a re-consecration, rather than the consecration of a new church. If it was a new church, it was not the first on the site: there had been one in the burgh for at least a century, probably longer. The teinds of the parish, levied on all agricultural produce and animals for the maintenance of the local church, also belonged to the Priory of St Andrews. Thus a considerable part of the burgh revenue – roughly a tenth – had already been diverted away from its purpose in order to support religious establishments outside the parish which were to become formidably rich, a pattern repeated throughout medieval Europe.

The Middle Ages knew no spelling orthodoxy; they reproduced the sounds of the language as best they could, and nowhere has this been more apparent than in the spelling of Linlithgow, which has had about two hundred variations. The name is said to mean 'loch in a damp hollow', from llyn (loch), laith (damp), and cau (a hollow). But etymology is a treacherous science. The name seems to have tried many writers, not least the English chronicler of Edward I's movements: "the viiith daie the Kynge went to his bedde to Lunsta" he wrote of one of his stopovers in the burgh.

The Terrible 14th Century

It is reasonable to assume that the burgh developed in the 12th and 13th centuries, following the general national expansion of the time. It is difficult, however, to overestimate the awfulness of 14th-century Europe, ridden with plague and warfare, which did not spare Scotland. The disputed succession of Alexander III (1241-1286) and of his granddaughter, Margaret, Maid of Norway, led to a long fight for independence from England. The burgh was unfortunately placed on the road from the capital to the stronghold of Stirling, probably one of the reasons for its origins. It was thus on the road to battles. Armies fed off the land, often brutally. The rules of war, such as they were, concerned the fighting class, the knights, and were irrelevant to peasants and tradesmen, whose goods were pillaged and lives easily sacrificed. The Scots operated a scorched earth policy against English armies, which resulted in misery largely hidden from history books: the locals were either pillaged by the enemy or burnt by the indigenous forces.

Edward I

Edward I (Langshanks) first appeared in Linlithgow in 1291, seeking to assert his sovereignty over Scotland. Lady Christina, Prioress of Manuel, swore fealty to him and others in the burgh probably did too. He reappeared in 1296, after the defeats of Berwick and Dunbar, when all the notables, including the bailies of Linlithgow, John Raebuck and John de Mar, and ten of its burgesses, pledged their allegiance. Edward had by then largely subdued southern Scotland and governed through local men, such as Archibald of Livingston, Sheriff of Linlithgow. In 1298, he was back, in pursuit of William Wallace; on 21st July he left Kirkliston for Linlithgow, where his army camped at the Burgh Muir to the east of the town; the following day he defeated Wallace at Falkirk.

In his attempt to subdue the country north of the Forth and Clyde, Edward spent the winter of 1301-1302 in Linlithgow, arriving on 28th October and leaving on 1st February to return to London. The 'King's chamber' had been upgraded for this visit by masons, smiths and thatchers, which suggest that the building was made of stone and straw. Extensive fortification works took place with the building of the peel, or palisade, made of split tree trunks. The promontory was isolated by a ditch and the palisade, enclosing the church which was used as a storehouse. A gatehouse stood at the centre with a bretasche, or wooden tower, at both ends of the loch. The works were conducted under the responsibility of Archibald of Livingston, who did something similar on a smaller scale at his Peel of Livingston, and the master of works was Master James de St George, who had had extensive experience of this type of fortification in Wales. The works lasted for two years, at the end of which Linlithgow was ready to be used as a supply base for Edward's operations in Stirling, for supply difficulties were his major weakness while in Scotland. From Linlithgow, the English army was provided with weapons and able to subdue the Scots at Stirling in 1304. The modern park called the Peel is the area that the medieval peel encircled.

Edward I was back in Linlithgow in June 1303 and again in August 1304, just before the Battle of Stirling which left him the master of Scotland. He departed Scotland for the last time thereafter leaving the garrison still in the peel, soon in the wardenship of a Gascon knight, Sir Piers de Luband, who controlled and owned much of the Lothians for the duration of the Wars of Independence.

Edward II

In his increasingly desperate attempts to oppose Robert Bruce, Edward II came to Scotland in 1310 and stayed in Linlithgow for two weeks in October. The journey achieved nothing. There is some argument as to the date on which the peel was liberated; the English exchequer accounts suggest that it was still in their hands at the time of the Battle of Bannockburn (1314) and that it was probably freed immediately after the battle. Barbour, in his *Bruce*, has a splendid story of a local farmer named William Bunnock, 'a stout carle and sture', who had a contract to supply hay to the garrison. He hid eight men in his hay cart and others were hidden nearby. On entering the gate, he used a pre-arranged signal, spread the hay and separated the horse from the cart, which made it impossible to close the drawbridge. The men emerged from the cart and their hideouts, subdued the garrison and occupied the peel. But, if they did, it cannot have been for very long - this is the stuff of epic tales, unconfirmed by any hard evidence. There is slight evidence, however, that the peel was besieged before Bannockburn, which is likely considering Bruce's guerilla tactics in the rest of the country, but it probably remained in English hands until the rout of 1314. All in all, the burgh had the enemy army, and sometimes the enemy king, on their doorstep for about a quarter of a century, a major impact on the lives of the townspeople.

After Bannockburn, the war continued south of the border until the Treaty of Edinburgh (1328) and resumed in 1332. Edward III fought repeatedly and to deadly effect from 1333 to 1337. The Scots resumed the scorched earth policy and the English pillaged randomly. In 1337, the English army set fire to Linlithgow. In a burgh built of wood, the result was catastrophic. The Knights Hospitallers (Knights of St John of Jerusalem), who owned many tenements in the burgh, reported that their "lands are burned and brought to nothing so that no revenue can be obtained from them, as a result of the prolonged and severe war in Scotland". The town is described as "uninhabited and totally waste". The war limped on until the English again devastated the Lothians in the 'Burnt Candlemas' of 1356 before signing the truce of the Treaty of Berwick in 1357.

The Charter

During the reign of David II (1329-1371), the Peel of Linlithgow was leased to John Cairns, Customar of the burgh, on condition that he should 'build the manor house' for the king's coming. Presumably the house was in a dilapidated state after all the fighting. Full rebuilding was probably not intended or possible; as for David II, his tormented reign was unlikely to leave him much time to pay attention to Linlithgow.

In 1349, the Black Death, the plague, which, it is reckoned, killed a third of the European population, reached Scotland. There were many other outbreaks in the following three centuries, although none as severe as this. Linlithgow was famous for being a healthy place, free from plague, and with healthy springs bringing it water. Time and again, the king, parliament and court took refuge from the plague in the burgh. Nevertheless they cannot have avoided it all the time (the king occasionally took refuge in such places as Aberdeen, which suggests that the south of Scotland was unsafe). The burgh took drastic measures to avoid letting plague carriers into the town, including installing gallows at the burgh ports.

The Exchequer records of the 14th century suggest that the trade of Linlithgow was among the busiest of the kingdom, a position from which it was to fall steadily over the centuries. In 1369, for example, the Linlithgow customs receipts far outstripped those of Stirling, Haddington, Aberdeen, Ayr, Perth or Dundee. In 1368, it became one of the burghs of the Court of the Four Burghs, as Roxburgh and Berwick had fallen into English hands in the endless Wars of Independence. It was given the custody of the standard grain measure, the boll (and its smaller measures, the firlot and peck). The 14th century was its high point in relative trading terms. Linlithgow could trade with northern Europe through its dedicated port of Blackness, which had the monopoly of shipping goods on the Firth of Forth from the mouth of the Avon to the mouth of the Almond. The overarching importance of Blackness contributed to the decline of the burgh when it lost out in the power battle with Bo'ness in the late 17th century, not least because of the influence of Duchess Anne at Kinneil.

In 1389, the burgh obtained its royal charter from Robert II, who spent much time there, an example of the general urban franchise movement of feudal Europe. The charter sums up concisely the privileges of the burgh: "Robert, by the grace of God, King of Scots, to all worthy men of his whole land, clerics and laymen, wisheth health; Know ye that we have granted and at ferme dimitted to our lovite and faithful burgesses and community of the Burgh of Lynlithcu, our Burgh aforesaid, together with the haven of Blaknes, the fermes of the Burgh, and petty customs and toll dues, with courts, and the issues of courts, and other just pertinents whatsoever: to be holden and had to our said burgesses and community aforesaid, and their successors, for ever... paying therefore to us and our heirs, the said burgesses and community, five pounds of sterlings every year, and at the usual terms... at Lithcu, the twenty third day of October, and of our reign the eighteenth year". The burgesses of Linlithgow were to guard their privileges jealously and take the 'for ever' at face value.

The Town Council

In 1540, the burgh was granted the right to elect a provost, a right which was to last until the 1975 local government reforms. It elected Henry Forrest of Magdalene as its first Provost. The Town Council was dominated by the merchant class, being made up of 27 members, including a provost, four bailies, a treasurer, and eight deacons elected by the guilds of craftsmen. 19 of the 27 members were therefore merchants. The Town Council members, and the bailies in particular, took themselves very seriously, expected respect, obedience and curtsies, all stated in local ordinances backed by stiff penalties. They were a self-selected body, drawn from a very narrow pool. Their election followed a tortuous opaque procedure by which burgesses, a privileged class in itself, were allowed to choose the council from a very short leet produced by the existing council. Of their later manifestation, Adam Dawson, himself a former provost, wrote: "In these days Provosts of Royal Burghs assumed much magisterial state. They were well-powdered, breeched, wore showy knee knuckles, and walked with long golden-headed canes. In Linlithgow, from four to six burgh officers, including the piper and the drummer, clothed in scarlet 'beefeater' coats of ample dimensions, trimmed with broad lace, having great cocked hats adorned with bows of ribbons, and bearing halberts, preceded the magistrates in their progress on public occasions. The Bailies had a strong opinion of their own power as judges, and sometimes went a little beyond constitutional law in dealing with delinquent vagrants. We once saw a woman drummed through the town with a turkey hanging to her neck, which she had stolen; and at another time, one with a pair of shoes that she had appropriated so attached, and so treated, doubtless, by a magistrate's order given at the shop door or behind the counter, without any formal trial. By the original constitution of the Royal Burgh, the town councils were elected by burgesses, which continued to be the case till certain of the later Stewarts ordained old councils to elect the new; and thus they became self-elected bodies. This state of things, in its working, rendered the provost master of the council, and made his seat one of much political value... Toryism was rampant in every burgh". The election of the council was so corrupt, with members of the same families continuing in power, that the burgh occasionally erupted in riots at the outcome. James Kirkwood, the Linlithgow school teacher who fought a long legal battle with the Town Council over his dismissal after the Revolution, famously satirised the magistrates as the '27 gods'.

In 1623, the council decided to elect a Dean of Guild and, in 1635, it set up a committee consisting of the Dean, four merchants and two craftsmen to assist the Dean. They regulated commercial activities within the burgh, held courts in maritime cases and in disputes between mariners and merchants, oversaw weights and measures, inspected hides and sheepskins at markets, dealt with general breaches of by-laws, regulated the admission of guild brothers, administered the guilds' charity funds and had exclusive privilege over staple and foreign commodities. They met weekly and were mostly concerned with preserving the burgh's trading privileges as well as charitable administration. By the mid 18th century, they dealt almost exclusively with boundary disputes and house maintenance. The Guildry House at Blackness was an imposing building providing warehousing and accommodation for merchants trading at the port, sadly pulled down in the destructive 1960s.

There were eight guilds in the burgh – the baxters (bakers), coopers, cordiners (shoemakers), fleshers (butchers), smiths, tailors, weavers and wrights, who elected their respective deacons to serve on the council. Apprentices, journeymen, craftsmen and masters were presided over by a deacon or dean, assisted by treasurers, a clerk and an officer, elected annually by the craftsmen. They operated a strict monopoly and regulated the trades (wages, apprentices, entry of strangers, quality of work and prices). The guilds supported altars in the unreformed church, and guarded their privileges jealously. Goods were displayed in booths projecting into the streets, while craftsmen worked behind the booth or in outbuildings. Servants and apprentices lived on the premises, forming compact human and economic units. Craftsmen registered their trademarks with the bailie court. There were also many unincorporated crafts, such as the dyers, tanners, glovers, pewterers, brewers, meal-makers, masons, sailors, candlemakers, slaters, stablers, carters, farmers, chapmen and horse-dealers. Many formed friendly societies and organised a form of poor relief for their members.

However corruptly elected it was, the burgh council seems to have run a tight ship, controlling the appearance and maintenance of buildings, organising the famous town wells, and maintaining welfare within the limited parameters of the times.

The Late Medieval Burgh

It is still possible to see the basic structure of the burgh as it emerged in the Middle Ages. The King's House, later the Palace, and the church dominated the town entirely. The Kirkgate, a busier road than at present, linked them to the single High Street where the townspeople lived. A series of vennels, including the Watergate, led from the loch side to the High Street and the Cross or market square which was the absolute centre of town life. The Tolbooth which preceded the present Burgh Halls was an all-purpose building: town hall, sheriff court, prison and shops. Timothy Pont's view of Linlithgow from the north shows a sketch of the Tolbooth as a very tall square building topped with an imposing weathervane. The Cross was the focal point of the burgh, where markets, fairs, trading, announcements, punishments and executions were conducted. Southeast of the church stood the Grammar School, at first a single room building. Next to the Tolbooth was the Fleshmarket. In the middle of the market square stood the symbol of the burgh, the Mercat Cross. This construction was destroyed in the early 19th century and was described from memory by the former Provost, Adam Dawson of Bonnytoun, who felt strongly about it: "The spirit of destruction was then actively at work in the demolition of the ancient Cross of the Burgh of Linlithgow, and of the West Port, for no reason that can be divined, unless for the gratification of the savage propensity alluded to... the structure containing the Cross, which stood so as to be visible from the outer porch of the palace-yard, and within a few yards of the line of the street, was an octagonal erection resting on a flight of steps, and surrounded with a bartizaned wall. In the centre, another building arose, which supported the sacred symbol. The space within the bartizan afforded room for the magistrates, town council, and principal inhabitants to assemble and 'drink the healths' on the King's birthday".

The burgh was accessed through its gates or 'ports'. At the east end were the East or High Port on the road to Edinburgh and the Low Port leading to Blackness. In the triangle between them stood the Middle Raw and the Chapel of the Blessed Virgin Mary, with its burial ground and almshouse. The gates guarded access to the burgh, enabling it to bar undesirables, eject those whom the bailies had banned from the burgh, control vagrants, sorners, beggars, and possible plague carriers. It also allowed control of customs and tolls. The south edge of the burgh was delineated by the town wall, which was not a fortification, but a simple low construction. Each resident of the south side was obliged to maintain a part of the wall at their 'yard-heads' to keep away the same undesirables and prevent evasion of petty customs. There were many complaints in council about the lack of diligence in the upkeep of the wall. Doors were allowed for private exit to the tail-riggs.

The herring-bone pattern of the old burgh largely remains: narrow fronted houses on both sides of the High Street with long back gardens or riggs, which, on the south side, ended at the yard-heads, or town wall. Slezer's view of the burgh from the south (see illustration opposite) shows the encircling wall, tidier than the real wall which was occasionally blown over by the wind. Behind the wall ran the South Vennel, which allowed the inhabitants to by-pass the High Street to reach Edinburgh and Bathgate. Also behind the wall, which followed roughly the line of the present railway line, were further strips of land, the tail-riggs, where the burgh could grow much of its food. Thus the High Street hid behind its façades a whole rural economy of outbuildings, crops and farm animals. At the west end of the High Street stood the West Port which controlled access from Bathgate and Falkirk, with another almshouse and the Chapel of St Ninian.

The Prospect of the Town of Linlithgow by Slezer.

The High Street itself was an uneven thoroughfare, narrow at the ports, widening at the Cross and narrowing again immediately west of the Cross. The street was unpaved; lined with manure heaps, galleries, arcades, booths, balconies and stairs fronting houses built higgledy-piggledy: the result must have been an unhealthy and pungent mess. The better classes avoided most of it by walking resolutely in the middle, raised part of the street, leaving the hoi polloi to walk and splash as best they could on the side.

Many of the houses would have been single-storey wooden hovels, which burnt quickly and were quickly rebuilt. But as the royal court spent more time in the burgh, the lords and lairds started keeping substantial townhouses or 'lodgings' in the proximity of the palace. Gradually, the southern part of the street around the Cross became dominated by these lodgings, none more imposing than the 'Great Inn', the house of the Earls of Linlithgow in the 17th century (roughly on the present site of the Royal Bank) or the lodging of Drummond of Hawthornden, which counted 14 hearths in 1691; Hamilton of Westport, by comparison, had only three, and the house of Cornwall of Bonhard, six. Nevertheless, the street remained a mixture of styles and classes: the Rosses of Halkhead, the Bishop of St Andrews, the Drummonds of Riccarton and Hawthornden, the Hamiltons of Pardovan, Westport, Kingscavil and just about everywhere else, lived next door to tailors, weavers, brewers, tanners and dyers.

The street ran firmly east-west, blocked at both ends by the ports. But this model could not function without the outlet of the wynds which gradually appeared – with changes of names, and earlier than has sometimes been stated – on the south side, to permit short cuts and allow the town to burst out of its medieval restrictions.

Slezer's *Prospect of the Town of Linlithgow*, though highly stylised, gives a good idea of the scale and pattern of the town in the latter half of the 17th century. Sir William Brereton, visiting Scotland in the 1630s commented on the town he called Light-Goaw: "This seems to be a fair, ancient town, and well built, some part of it in stone. Here is a fair church and a dainty conduit in the middle of the street" (the Cross Well erected in 1628).

The Church

It is difficult to overestimate the importance of ecclesiastical establishments in the medieval burgh. Apart from St Michael's, the Chapel of the Blessed Virgin Mary in the Middle Raw and St Ninian's Chapel at the West Port, there were, amongst others, the Carmelite friary established around 1401 on the south side; religious almshouses at various times in the Kirkgate, the Low Port and the Middle Raw; a hospital or leper house dedicated to St Magdalene, firmly outside the town gates; and the nunnery of Manuel on the banks of the Avon. St Michael's was not only a church, it was an economic unit, with a network of numerous altars supported contractually by guilds and individuals. The church did not hesitate to enforce the contracts. In addition, abbeys and monasteries owned vast chunks of the burgh. The Priory of St Andrews owned the teinds for several centuries, a considerable source of revenue, and the Prioress of Manuel owned the burgh mills at a time when thirlage (the obligation of tenants and feuars to grind their grain at particular mills) was rigorously enforced. The Knights of St John in Torphichen owned the 'Temple Lands' (the term generally described not only the lands they had inherited from the dissolved Templar Order, but their own). A rental of 1540 identifies 20 properties in the High Street as Temple lands. Their Linlithgow headquarters were probably in the building known as 'the Mint', destroyed in 1885, which stood a few steps down from the present railway station.

The Linlithgow Apogee: The 15th and 16th Centuries

The fires of 1411 and 1424 destroyed much of the town. By coincidence, 1424 also saw the return of James I from eighteen years in exile as the hostage of the King of England. Back in his kingdom, he set about building the Palace, which still stands, and the reconstruction of the church, which may not have been completely destroyed by the fire. James' project was political - he was showing off; the Palace was a fitting setting for a new kind of ruler and law-maker, the centre for a grand court, an assertion of his (misplaced) confidence. The Palace was inspired by the buildings of England and France where he had spent much of his youth. The project started in 1425 and cost a fortune, all itemised in the Treasurer's Accounts. The presence of the grand new palace strengthened the association of the burgh with the Stewarts which ended with James VI's departure for London in 1603. It was conceived as a place of courtly grace and pleasure. It became the property of dowager Stewart queens. Here, for example, Sir David Lindsay's *Satire of the Three Estates* was first performed for James V's court (1540). The Palace which James I built was much altered over the centuries but its basic plan survives. James IV upgraded the royal apartments on the west side, built a new chapel and a turreted barbican on the east side, where the entrance used to be. James V upgraded it for his first wife and presented it to his second, Mary of Guise, who admired it greatly. Her admiration was not diplomatic, the palace was built to continental standards of sophistication. James Hamilton of Finnart had moved the entrance to the south side, built the outer gateway, refurbished the great hall, built a new fountain and installed a tennis court.

The brightest star in the Stewart line was probably James IV. Before the battle of Flodden (9th September 1513), a ghost appeared to the king at prayer in St Katherine's Aisle in St Michael's Church, warning him against going to war, before disappearing as mysteriously as it had appeared. What happened? The general consensus is that this was a trick got up by the Queen, Margaret Tudor. The Queen, Henry VIII's sister, is said to have waited in vain for the King's return from Flodden in the look-out post above the north-west turnpike stair, now known as 'Queen Margaret's Bower'. Whatever the truth of these tales, they carry the sense of desolation which followed the killing field that was Flodden.

The Hamilton Century

A 16th-century writer commenting on West Lothian called it 'Hamiltoun countrie'. The family dominated the county. There were many of them, with the same limited range of first names, a lot of them illegitimate, which makes them difficult to disentangle. They had extensive lands in West Lothian, from the large barony of Livingston in the south to Abercorn and the lands and Palace of Kinneil in the north. Many of them had lodgings in Linlithgow. The notaries' protocol books are full of their legal transactions, notably the books of the ubiquitous Thomas Johnstoun who lived and worked in the burgh from 1520 to 1570 as notary, priest, and Town Clerk: a man with a long life and apparently formidable energy.

The first Lord Hamilton had married Mary, sister of James II, and thus his descendants were heir to the throne should the fragile Stewart royal house fail (a real possibility: most of them inherited the throne as children, fell in the hands of one or other faction of the Scottish nobility and died young; James V's famous phrase: "it cam' wi' a lass, it will gang wi' a lass" was a realistic appraisal). The importance of the successive heads of the Hamilton clan - the Lords Hamilton, then Earls of Arran, Duke of Chatelherault, Dukes of Hamilton in the 17th century - was only equalled by the pathetic weakness, vacillation, greed and general inadequacy which characterised all of them, not to mention the outright madness of one of them. Nevertheless, they made up in quantity what they lacked in quality. Much of what happened to Linlithgow in the 16th century can be explained by their presence in their West Lothian strongholds, and it is entirely suitable that the oldest surviving houses in the burgh should be Hamilton's Land, built in the 16th century for Hamilton of Pardovan, and West Port House, for Hamilton of Silvertounhill.

The first of these notable events was the 1526 Battle of Linlithgow Bridge. This was a familiar struggle between the nobles of Scotland for power and control of the child king James V, in particular between the Angus faction and the Hamiltons. The Queen Dowager, supported by the Earl of Arran and the Earl of Moray, gathered a force at Linlithgow in January 1526 to oppose the Earl of Angus who held the King. The Queen and Moray failed to turn up and Arran, typically, decided not to risk doing anything, disbanded his army and fled. On 4th September of that year, there was a repeat. Lennox and an army of some 10,000 men met on the bridge over the Avon, which was barred by Arran, who, typically, had changed sides. Lennox retreated to Manuel Haugh opposite the Manuel nunnery, was defeated and surrendered to Hamilton of Pardovan. The cruel and brilliant James Hamilton of Finnart killed him against all the rules of war and the tradition of Scottish armies. 'Lennox's Cairn', now relocated at the entrance of Kettilstoun Mains, commemorates the deed.

In 1540, Hamilton of Finnart 'ane of the Kingis maist familiare counselleris and servitouris', Master of the King's Works, who had revamped the palace for the arrival of James V's new queen, and had been master of the works at St Michael's, lost the favour of the king, who, it is said, wanted his fortune, and was accused of treason. Among the heads of accusation, he was charged with having fired at the king from the Linlithgow Tolbooth campanile. He was swiftly executed.

The 1540s probably saw the apogee of the burgh. Mary Queen of Scots was born like her father in the palace, on 8th December 1542. For this most famous of all 'black bitches', the magistrates busied themselves removing vagrants from the town, who might have been responsible for the infant queen's attack of smallpox (strangers are always responsible for misfortunes). Mary spent the first nine months of her life in the palace and rarely put her foot in the place again. During her personal reign in the 1560s, she only used the palace for quick stopovers. James Hamilton, 2nd Earl of Arran, heir presumptive to the throne in the likely event of the infant Queen's death, became Governor of the kingdom. He wavered, in the Hamilton way, from English to French allegiance which provoked Henry VIII into the years of destruction in Lothian known as the 'Rough Wooing'. Edinburgh was burnt, the plague raged, and the Court, the Governor, and anybody who was anybody, took refuge in Linlithgow. Arran installed himself in the Palace from 1544. The Court of Session came, tax collectors came, so did burgh representatives, Members of Parliament, sheriffs, stewarts, bailies, and aldermen. They all lived in the town, which must have been very crowded and very busy. In 1554, Arran resigned his governorship, Mary of Guise became Regent, and Scotland was about to embark on the trauma of the Reformation. French troops, who occupied the country during her regency, made occasional sorties in and around Linlithgow, and 'spoiled all the country'. On 29th June 1559, the Protestant leaders came to Linlithgow, in the wake of similar actions in Perth, Stirling and elsewhere, and purged the church of the apparatus of medieval worship. Thus the church lost almost all its statues and altars, regarded as idolatrous objects. Fragments from this destruction occasionally surface around the church ground, revealing some of the beauty which had adorned the parish church.

The Murder of Regent Moray

The Hamiltons were also responsible for the most notorious event in the whole history of the town: the assassination of Regent Moray by James Hamilton of Bothwellhaugh. In its historical context, Linlithgow became the Dallas of its time, the place where the most powerful man in the land was murdered. James Stewart, Earl of Moray, was one of James V's numerous bastards, an able man who had served well his irritating half-sister, Mary, for a period when it suited him. Mary's reign had been badly derailed on her marriage to Darnley, his murder at Kirk o' Field in Edinburgh, and her marriage to Bothwell. Imprisoned and forced to resign in favour of her son soon after his birth, she had managed to escape, but lost the Battle of Langside in 1568, where most of the Hamilton clan had fought on her side. They had forfeited their lands and positions as a result. By 1570, the country was divided into the 'King's Party', which supported James VI, and the 'Queen's Party' (there was not the simplistic Catholic/Protestant distinction often described; the Hamiltons, for example, were Protestant). Moray, probably one of the ablest men of his time, and the King's uncle, had become Regent of Scotland.

In late January 1570, he stopped overnight in Linlithgow on his way back to Edinburgh. He stayed in a lodging in the select part of the High Street, slightly east of the Dog Well Wynd, possibly the house of Drummond of Riccarton. Moray had hoped to attack Dumbarton Castle held by the Flemings on behalf of the Queen, and realising that it could not be done, was making his way back through Glasgow and Stirling. His assassin, James Hamilton of Bothwellhaugh, had tried to kill him already in both these places. The Regent and his entourage were therefore very aware of the danger. There were many contemporary discussions about Bothwellhaugh's motives: had his wife been ill-treated and killed on the Regent's orders? Were his motives personal or political? The question had little meaning to the Hamiltons and the men of their time: the personal and the political were identical. Bothwellhaugh was one of these psychopaths who flourished in troubled times. (After his triumph in Linlithgow, he escaped to the Continent where he was implicated in attempts on the life of the French Protestant Admiral Coligny and several plots against the Prince of Orange. He became a professional hitman.)

Bothwellhaugh was given the use of a house belonging to John Hamilton, Archbishop of St Andrews, a few houses away from where Moray was staying, and made very elaborate preparations. He had serious tactical problems, since nobody was going to let him get anywhere near the Regent, so that a quick old-fashioned attack with a sword was out of the question. He had to kill from a distance. This turned out to be a very modern murder, the first assassination with a hand-held gun. He used a hackbut, the most powerful hand weapon of the time, which functioned like a cannon. It was also unwieldy and heavy; it needed loading with powder, wadding, and bullets. A match had to be set to the powder, and firing produced a serious recoil which could badly derail the trajectory of the bullets.

The Archbishop's house (see page 13) stood on the location of the present Sheriff Court and was set back from the High Street. It had a wide gallery fronting the street which Bothwellhaugh was said to have covered with linen in order to conceal himself. The walls of the front room were lined with black to eliminate shadows: all appearance of a presence on the frontage had to be eliminated. The floor was covered with feather mattresses to deaden the sound of his boots, and a small hole was pierced in the linen for the shot. Another problem was the route which the Regent was going to take on leaving his lodgings after spending the night in Linlithgow. The obvious way was to proceed east along the High Street towards the High Port. But his entourage was nervous, and, anxious to avoid the obvious, apparently decided to turn west to go by the back way, through the Dog Well Wynd, along the South Vennel, and thence to Edinburgh, as was fairly commonly done. The High Street at this point was at its narrowest, with busy traffic and all manner of encumbrances lining the path, a bodyguard's nightmare.

Bothwellhaugh had anticipated this, and stuffed the wynd with brushwood which blocked the paths of the riders in the Regent's party. They backtracked into the High Street and passed the Archbishop's house. Bothwellhaugh fired. Moray was hit below the navel, the bullet going right through his body, but he was apparently able to go back to his lodgings, where he died a slow death during the night of 23rd January (incredibly, the plaque on the site gets the date wrong). His body was taken to Edinburgh and buried in the south aisle of St Giles' Church, the elderly John Knox pronouncing the funeral oration. It was a great solemn occasion.

Bothwellhaugh had more logistical problems: he had to escape fast. He had planned this part carefully, parking his already-saddled horse, borrowed from John Hamilton, Abbot of Arbroath, behind the Archbishop's house. The house, like all those on the south side of the street, had a long rigg or garden at the back bordered by the town wall, with a door too small for a horse and rider. He had taken care to remove the lintel stone in order to escape at great speed on horseback. He rode furiously towards his natural territory, Hamilton in Lanarkshire.

All hell broke loose. English troops under Sir William Drury crossed the border to take revenge on the Hamiltons, who had undoubtedly aided and abetted the deed. They burnt and destroyed the Hamilton lands in Clydesdale and West Lothian, starting with the Palace and town of Hamilton, then such properties as the Peel of Livingston, Binny, Park and Kingscavil, ending up with the Palace of Kinneil. The mood was ugly. Linlithgow should have been the prime target for destruction, and, according to a chronicler, Drury gave the people of the town hours to clear their infirm and children before the town burnt. He acceded, however, to the pitiful supplications of the people and spared the town, reserving his destruction for Arran's house. Whether or not the house of Archbishop Hamilton survived is not clear, but the Archbishop did not: he was executed the following year along with some servants. Like most acts of violence, it solved nothing. Linlithgow became the headquarters of the Queen's Party; the civil war intensified and lasted for another three years, but the Queen's Party, on whose behalf all this had been done, was already doomed. Bothwellhaugh was never again successful in his career as an assassin of high profile figures; he was never again to find himself in the bosom of a large clan prepared to shield him in their heartland.

Nothing remotely like this happened in Linlithgow again. The burgh was approaching its long decline with the end of the Stewarts' residence in Scotland in 1603, losing its role as a power base. The heady days of the 1540s were over. In 1585, when James VI started his personal reign, and again in the 1590s, a time of crop failure, dearth, and plague as well as political strife, the court and parliament moved to the burgh for long periods. But it took James VI's personal and only visit back to Scotland in 1617 eventually to make him aware that the north wall of the palace was falling down. This led to the rebuilding of the north range into one of the finest façades of Renaissance Scotland. In 1600, Henri, Duc de Rohan, had professed himself unimpressed with Linlithgow, but felt obliged to mention it as he had met the king's daughter there (Elizabeth, later Queen of Bohemia, who was educated in the household of the Earl of Linlithgow). With the removal of the Court, and later of Edinburgh as a seat of government, people unimpressed with Linlithgow no longer had to visit it! The power of the Hamiltons waned, to be replaced in the area by the ascendant Livingstons, Earls of Linlithgow, but the centre of real power had moved to London. Linlithgow settled down to a quieter life, until the nadir described in *Dreamthorp* (see below).

In 1633, Charles I, on official visit for his coronation in Scotland, proceeded on a slow stately march through his northern kingdom, accompanied by his Court and an endless train of luggage for which hundreds of horses from all the parishes of West Lothian had been gathered to cover the Holyrood to Linlithgow stretch. The Town Council was thrown into a fever of preparation for this visit. On 1st July, the King stayed for the last time in his fair palace, its last royal guest.

Religious Troubles

The burgh was naturally involved in the religious strife which saw the country change from a Catholic to a profoundly Presbyterian nation, followed by the various schisms of the Reformed Church.

The most dramatic event heralding the agitation for reform was the martyrdom of Patrick Hamilton in 1528. Patrick was an aristocrat, one of the numerous Hamilton tribe which ruled much of West Lothian. He was the son of Sir Patrick Hamilton of Kingscavil, who was the natural son of the first Lord Hamilton and the brother of the first Earl of Arran. Sir Patrick, described as a model of Scottish chivalry, had died in 1520 in the unseemly brawl in Edinburgh High Street between the Hamiltons and the Douglases, known as 'Cleanse the Causeway'. His mother was Catherine Stewart, the daughter of Alexander, Duke of Albany, the brother of James III. In 1517, Patrick became titular abbot of Fearn, in Ross-shire, where he probably never set foot: part of the corruption of the old church was the way religious benefices – which were enormous – had been diverted to secular purposes and in particular to the great families of the kingdom. He had been educated in the universities of Paris and Louvain, before joining the University of St Andrews, where the ideas of Luther were circulating. So much so that an Act of 1525 banned these ideas and, in early 1527, Patrick took refuge in Marburg, where he developed and expounded his theology (*Patrick's Places*). His central thesis of the justification by faith alone, and the place of good works in a man's life, was straight Lutheran theology. In late 1527, he returned to Scotland, with the intention of preaching the reformed ideas in his native land. He seems to have settled in Kingscavil and preached on his brother's extensive lands in West Lothian. He was a serious intellectual young man (born around 1504). His proselytising soon reached the ears of the Catholic authorities and he was asked to account for himself by Archbishop Beaton in St Andrews. Very quickly, so that his brother could not mount a rescue of armed men, he was condemned and burnt in a horrifyingly lingering death in front of St Salvator's College on 29th February 1528. His preaching ministry in and around Linlithgow had lasted just a few months. The Linlithgow Augustinian friar, Henry Forrest, was also martyred there in 1533.

The reformed ideas would have spread not only through universities but also through the ports trading with northern Europe and the merchant class of Linlithgow and Blackness

The house from which Hamilton of Bothwellhaugh is thought to have shot Regent Moray - engraving by Philippe de la Motte.

would be exposed to them (the 1525 Act specifically prohibited the import of Lutheran books by ships).

The Linlithgow Grammar School teacher at the time of the Reformation (1560) was the celebrated priest Ninian Winzet, whose scholastic and debating skills were widely admired. He argued for the internal reform of the old church and stood by his Catholicism, which in the end cost him his job at the school (1561). Winzet had obviously enjoyed the 'kindly town' of Linlithgow, from where he exiled himself to Italy. Thus the burgh had nurtured two of the leading figures of the period, on both sides of the argument, which reflected its importance at the crossroads of the nation, something which would not be repeated; a reputation for intellectual debate is not a feature of the later burgh (see *Dreamthorp* below). Two notable Protestant martyrs had come from Linlithgow.

The debates after the Reformation, apart from the degree of Catholic repression, centred on the nature of the reformed church, broadly Episcopalian or Presbyterian, and the degree of royal control, issues which would continue until the 1689 Revolution and the settlement embodied in the Act of Union (1707).

The 17th Century

The battle raged most fiercely with the National Covenant (1638) which was signed by practically everybody – copies of the Linlithgowshire covenant have survived, with the forceful central signatures of the Dalyells of the Binns, father and son, and most of the landowners of West Lothian. The 1640s saw the arch-Presbyterian ascendancy, the Taliban of their time, with the power of the Committee of Estates, taking over from the King, increasing religious and social tyranny and the enforcement of a new orthodoxy through the kirk sessions and presbytery as well as the burgh courts.

But while parliamentary forces were gaining ground in England, Montrose and his royalist Highland and Irish forces were blazing through Scotland in a string of brilliant victories over Covenanting armies. In February 1645, he won the Battle of Kilsyth and was getting dangerously near the capital and submission of lowland Scotland. Frightened for their life and property, the heritors of the county and burgesses went to Kilsyth, with their tail between their legs, and acknowledged their submission to Montrose, a form of insurance policy: saving the town from destruction warranted any amount of crawling to the Master of Napier. On his way to Philiphaugh, Montrose trailed through West Lothian, helping himself to 'donations' from the people such as food, clothing and horses. It was the old tactic of living from the land, which had cost so much in the 14th century wars. Defeated in August at Philiphaugh, Montrose fled the country, his cause lost. The Covenanters took their revenge, with massacres of the defeated soldiers and camp followers, including, according to rumour and Sir George MacKenzie, eighty women and children thrown into the Avon over the bridge at Linlithgow. The church made the people pay for their sins by ordering them stand on the pillar of repentance in the kirks, acknowledging their weakness in helping Montrose.

The heady atmosphere of civil war, together with the increased religious control of the presbyteries, the several bad harvests and the plagues of 1644-46 which followed the armies, is hard at this distance to imagine, with its poverty, disease, war and religious hysteria. It is in this context of heightened tension and misery that we must place the episode of witchcraft in Linlithgow as well as the numerous others in West Lothian. There had been serious outbreaks of witchhunting in 1643 and 1644 in Mid Calder and Queensferry, Abercorn and Bo'ness, in

1647 in Livingston and in 1648 in Carriden and Linlithgow. 1649, a terrible year in the fortunes of Scotland, saw serious outbreaks all over southern Scotland, in particular in Queensferry, Dalmeny, Carriden and Kirkliston.

On 1st March 1648, the Presbytery records mention that "Nanse Dunlop in Linlithgow is accused of witchcraft". On 11th March, she confessed to her acts of witchcraft. In the intervening period, the elders and burgesses of the burgh would have taken it in turn to 'wake' her (to keep her awake), a well-tried form of torture. Her confession is a classic catalogue of the known manifestations of witchcraft as it was understood at the time: submission to the devil, devil's marks on the body, satanic servants in the shape of black cats, sexual intercourse with the devil, Satan's promises of riches, cursing and 'charming', responsibility for harming local individuals and renunciation of baptism. She is said to have lived in a house located on the present site of the Four Marys pub, where the devil visited her "at twilicht in hir yaird at the backhous end". What triggered the accusation of sorcery? She had the stereotypical profile of the average witch of the period: she was old – in her mid sixties – and poor. She compounded her crime by confessing to an adulterous relationship as a young woman and conspiring with her lover to kill her baby, for which he was executed, but she was spared. She may have had a bad reputation. Several witches called Dunlop had been executed in West Lothian in the past decades, and it was well known that sorcery ran in families. Whatever it was, her "friely uncompelled" confession of witchcraft in front of the minister and four bailies of the town would have sealed her fate. The council detailed the expense of burning her (£12 17s 2d for six barrels of firewood, one tar barrel, tow and rope, hemp for making a jupp, payment to the executioner; presumably she did not have relatives from whom they could have recovered these outlays, nor did her possessions cover it). Others were accused in the burgh but seem to have escaped the stake.

Cromwell

On 3 September 1650, Cromwell defeated the Scots at Dunbar and strove to occupy and subdue Scotland. Linlithgow found itself back in its strategic position of 1301 in the battlefield triangle of central Scotland. Cromwell entered the town on 9th October 1650, spent some of the winter there and, for the same reasons as Edward I before him, installed himself in the Palace, garrisoned his troops in the peel and his horses in the church. But the Palace was no more fortified than the old royal house, so back came the fortifications for which he needed extensive materials: the easiest method was to lift the stones of the buildings in the Kirkgate, the almshouse there, the Tolbooth, the schoolhouse and the manse. The Council had bravely retreated to Culross for the duration and the burgh records were taken hostage and chased throughout Scotland. The population splintered along politico-religious lines (Protesters and Resolutioners) and worshipped at either end of the literally partitioned church.

After the Restoration, much rebuilding took place at the Cross and Kirkgate, most notably of the Town House, rebuilt to a plan by Robert Milne, the King's mason, and completed in 1670, in time to figure prominently on Slezer's 1678 view of the town from the south (illustration on page 9).

Restoration

Linlithgow expressed its relief at the end of the Covenanting regime and the restoration of Episcopacy by publicly burning the Covenant at the Cross on 29th May 1662, the King's birthday, in a bizarre ceremony which involved (wicked) French wine flowing in the fountain and many bonfires. Later Puritan writers, horrified at this shame on the honour of the town, have suggested that this was entirely the responsibility of the Provost, Andrew Glen, the bailies, the minister, who later became a bishop, and the local magnate and hereditary Keeper of the Palace, the Earl of Linlithgow. Certainly, this celebration could not have taken place without the sanction of the local authorities, but it is difficult to gauge how much the town actually rejoiced. When the wind had turned again in the 1690s, the Town Council denied any role in the affair.

In the following decades, the battle over the form of church government intensified. The people of West Lothian were actively involved in conventicles where dissenters, deserting the legal church, gathered to worship. The extensive moors of the county provided convenient eerie sites for large gatherings, while Bo'ness seems to have harboured increasingly wild and extreme forms of religious cults. The burgh and sheriff court records list hundreds of people fined for their conventicling. Militia troops were quartered in the town in the 1670s. In 1675, the Grammar School teacher David Skeoch was sacked for non-conformity and replaced by James Kirkwood, who, apart from teaching the Grammar School pupils, seems to have had enough resources to lend considerable sums to the Town Council. In 1679, following the defeat of the extreme Covenanting factions at Bothwell Bridge, prisoners passed through Linlithgow in a desolate state, hungry, unclothed, and were herded in the Fleshmarket. Matters came to a head in 1681 when the increasingly beleaguered Privy Council set about enforcing the Test Act, by which all officials had to swear allegiance to the King and adhere to the religious dispensation. George Livingston, Third Earl of Linlithgow, decided to make his home town of Linlithgow toe the line.

Livingston Family

The Livingston family had moved up in the world slowly and surely over the centuries. They originated from the 12th-century Leving who had settled his farmtoun in a bend of the Almond, Livingstoun. The last Livingston of that ilk had died in obscurity in 1512, but the Linlithgow branch had prospered, becoming wealthy merchants in the burgh and being elevated to Court positions. In 1450, the family paid, some with their lives, for their shady role during the minority of James II. Returned to favour, James Livingston of Callendar, the king's chamberlain, became the First Lord Livingston. The family became more and more closely associated with the Stewarts. In 1542, the Fifth Lord was appointed guardian of the infant Queen, and his daughter Mary was one of the famous four Marys. The Sixth Lord fought at Langside on Mary's side in 1568. The Seventh Lord was created First Earl of Linlithgow in 1599 and became a member of the Privy Council and hereditary Keeper of the Palace. In 1681, the Third Earl descended on the town of Linlithgow, where he maintained his splendid lodgings, and asked all members of the council to swear the Test on their knees. The provost, Alexander Milne, resigned, the earl's son was appointed provost and, for five years, all municipal liberties in the town were suspended while the Livingstons reigned supreme, a source of great local resentment. The Fourth Earl fought with Claverhouse at Killiecrankie, and the Fifth Earl showed his loyalty to the Stewarts by commanding a squadron at the Battle of Sheriffmuir, which ended the 1715 Jacobite campaign. His lands and titles were forfeited and that was the end of the Livingston Earls of Linlithgow.

After the Revolution, the world was turned upside down again. James Kirkwood was kicked out of his school for Episcopalian sympathies, his fine Dutch furniture piled in the street. He embarked on the long legal battle with the council, which included a satirical pamphlet entitled *The History of the Twenty Seven Gods of Linlithgow*, a vitriolic attack on the members of the Town Council. Kirkwood, a clever man with a good reputation, was the author of several Latin grammars and had a good opinion of himself, only equalled by his contempt for the town magistrates. In 1712, he eventually won his legal battle.

The 18th Century

The hearth tax records of 1691 show a town of about 2,500 inhabitants with 594 declared hearths, a substantial number of them in the great houses on the south side of the High Street. The back yards housed a network of kilns, stables, tanning pits, malt barns, not to mention the doocot of the Rosses of Halkhead. In the early 1700s, the writer and spy Daniel Defoe travelled through the burgh and wrote of a "pleasant, handsome, well-built town; the tolbooth is a good building, and not old, kept in good repair, and the streets clean. The people look here as if they were busy, and had something to do whereas in most towns we pass through they seemed as if they look disconsolat for want of employment. The whole Green, fronting the lough or lake, was covered with linnen-cloth, it being the bleaching season, and I believe a thousand women and children, and not less, tending and managing the bleaching business; the town is served with water by one very large basin, or fountain, to which the water is brought from the same spring which served the royal palace. At Lithgow there is a very great Linnen Manufacture as there is at Glasgow; and the water of the Lough here is esteemed with the best in Scotland for bleaching and whitening of linnen cloth, so that a great deal of linnen made in other parts of the country is brought here to be bleach'd or whiten'd". The population of Scotland at the time was underemployed, which would have hurt Defoe's utilitarian instincts, and it is interesting to note that Linlithgow seemed different, and busy. The linen production was of long standing in the burgh; the bleachfield was important enough for the Armstrong map of the 1770s to show it as a vast expanse west of the loch.

Life was nevertheless always hard for most of the inhabitants and teetered into famine when bad harvests led to high grain prices. There had been no unrest during the terrible lean years of 1695-1700, when people died of starvation and the diseases of hunger. In the following century, there were occasional riots, for example in February 1720 when an angry crowd rounded on members of the council as they left Sunday service and beat up the town officers. A largely submissive population occasionally erupted in anger in the streets. In 1725, the Jacobite George Carnwath rubbed his hands in glee at the idea of the Advocate General's workload: "As Lord Ilay seems to thirst after bloody processes, he's like to get work enuff, for there hath been a great mob at Linlithgow about choosing the magistrates and sevrall are takn up and to be tryd". These popular movements forced the Town Council to hold intervention stores, which suggest that they had been seriously scared by mobs (the Old Statistical Account mentions a warehouse containing 600 bolls of meal for times of scarcity). Adam Dawson records such an occasion: "Dearths from bad harvests then appear to have been frequent, and for one of these visitations a 'meal mob' resolved to make Mr James Andrew, brewer, Linlithgow, the provost [1786-1802] responsible, and sought his life; but while the mob entered his premises, he escaped by the back way, mounted his horse, and fled into the country, where he remained till the wrath of the people were appeased by the establishment of a 'girnal' from which meal was dolled out to the hungry at an undervalue".

The council complained on a regular basis of the competition in trading which encroached on their monopolies. The town never recovered its 14th-century dominance in this area. In the 17th century, Bo'ness, Grangepans, Kirkliston, Torphichen, Bathgate, Queensferry and other places were made burghs of barony, with trading rights. The customs house at Blackness was moved to Bo'ness, a further nail in the coffin. The council complained of this situation to the Convention of Royal Burghs in 1692 and at regular intervals thereafter: "Ther forraigne trade, both of export and import is very inconsiderable and they have no inland trade in gross except about 10,000 weight of tallow and 1600 or 1800 sheep skines or thereby yearly... they have no ships, barks, boats, or ferrie boats belonging to them. They have only five or six of ther burgers and inhabitants that have interests in ships". There were by then six annual fairs lasting two days and a weekly market which had been moved from Saturday to Friday in order to allow the inhabitants to appear sober on the Sabbath. By the 18th century, the burgh had settled down to being a small town of craftsmen, artisans and local traders.

In 1745, the burgh was yet again in the path of opposing armies. On Sunday 15th September, Charles Edward Stuart and his Highland army reached the town which was about to attend Sunday service. The Provost, John Bucknay, a Jacobite sympathiser, left town for the duration. Mrs Glen Gordon, who occupied the palace, organised celebrations, with wine flowing from the fountain, while the soldiers pillaged the High Street. The army camped at St Magdalene's, then moved to stay at Threemiletown, the Prince staying at Kingscavil House before proceeding to Edinburgh. The town may have celebrated and welcomed the Prince, but it had few real Jacobite supporters prepared to join the rebel army. After the retreat from Derby, the Jacobite army reappeared under Lord George Murray on 13 January 1746. General Hawley, commanding the Government forces, briefly occupied the Palace before and after his defeat at Falkirk. The Duke of Cumberland next appeared on his way north and the number of troops at Linlithgow reached 10,000. A contingent quartered in the palace left fires carelessly unextinguished and the old curse of the Middle Ages, fire, spread as they left, on 1st February. It is fittingly symbolic that the palace of the Stewarts should have become a ruin just as the Stewart cause was about to be lost forever.

Robert Burns visited the town in 1787 to see his friend Alexander Smith who ran a calico mill at Linlithgow Bridge. His view of the town, much quoted, is evoked with a few words in his diary: "Linlithgow, the appearance of rude, decayed, idle grandeur, charmingly rural, retired situation. The old rough palace a tolerably fine but a melancholy ruin". The 'decayed idle grandeur' is a beautiful apposite phrase, which can still describe the town.

Leather

The leather industry is what Linlithgow is rightly famous for: it dominated the burgh for several centuries, and visitors can obtain much information about it in the local High Street museum, Annet House. Local tradition has it that the English soldiers introduced the craft to the burgh during the Cromwellian occupation. The 1620 records of the Scottish Privy Council mention a complaint to the effect that tanning in the town was of a very low standard, and the councillors decided to import some English tanners to teach the locals. Unfortunately, the Privy Council's decisions had as much to do with wishful thinking as direct action. The administration was too weak to execute its own orders. So this particular decision may have been implemented, or maybe not. But somehow, sometime during the course of the 17th century, the craft was transformed from self-sufficient amateurishness to well defined crafts and techniques. The shoemakers who used to tan their own leather gave way to a division of crafts: tanners, curriers, tawers and shoemakers. There were plenty of hides in the local parishes, and plenty of water around. The smells can be left to the imagination.

In 1795, the local minister, Reverend James Dobie, wrote: "The manufacture of leather is the most extensive and advantageous carried on here. There are employed in it 17 tanners, 18 curriers, and 13 tawers", adding that shoemaking is the "chief branch of the trade here" with 100 people employed in it. They used to export to America, before the War of Independence, and Lord Hopetoun had relieved difficult times in the industry by ordering 700 pairs of boots for the army fighting the Napoleonic wars, an example of enlightened and generous patronage in his eyes. This suggests a serious depression in the latter half of the century.

Fifty years later, the Reverend Andrew Bell wrote: "The leather trade, in its various branches, may be called the staple of the town. It is said to have been introduced by the soldiers of Cromwell. There are 23 master boot and shoemakers, employing 276 journeymen, and 43 apprentices. The wages of the former are 10s per week, and of the latter 3s. Thirty women are also employed as women's boot-binders, whose weekly wages average 4s 6d. There are five master tanners, employing 28 men in this trade, the rate of the wages is determined by the skill of the workmen. A tanner, bred to the employment, receives 13s per week, while the average wages of what are called labouring tanners, that is, men not brought up to the work, are only 9s. The master curriers amount to nine, employing about 50 men, whose average rate of wages is 14s per week. In the shoe trade, the hours are long – from six to six, and often later. In the currying branch of the trade, the men work only ten hours a day. The tanning and currying departments are in a prosperous condition, and the shoemakers are well employed. There was a temporary depression in the last-named trade some time back, but it has again revived".

The shoemakers (cordiners) were one of the eight long-established incorporated trades of the town, and the town's architecture still bears the marks of this guild (see page 70).

The Old Statistical Account

The Old Statistical Account, written in 1795 by the new minister, Mr James Dobie, gives a good idea of the economic life of the town: "The street, towards the east, is broad and airy; about the middle, contracted and gloomy; as one goes westward, it again enlarges itself. Many of the houses have, it must be owned, a mean aspect and exhibit striking symptoms of decay. Several, however, have lately been rebuilt, the whole may be expected to assume a modern and more elegant appearance... even the old houses have their effect on the contemplative mind. As many of these, during the Royal residence at Linlithgow, belonged to persons of the first rank, they mark the simplicity of former time". He reminds us that a Scottish town was always half rural: "The inhabitants are chiefly supplied with milk and butter by people in the town, who keep from 1 to 3 cows. The number in all amounts to 108. Many of these have little pasture, and are fed with grains or boiled meat". Leather and Shoemaking dominated, but he also identifies one carpet weaver, 23 stocking framers, ten of them employed by a Glasgow company. "Two tambour [embroidery] factories were lately erected here. The one employs 36 girls, who are bound for three years, and have 1s 6d a week the first year, 2s the second, and 2s 6d the third.

At the other, 50 are engaged for the same time, who receive 2d more a week. The companies at Glasgow for who they are employed allow an annual sum for instructing them in the principles of religion: with that view, attendance is given every Lord's Day by two teachers in town". The linen manufacturing noticed by Defoe had totally disappeared following the introduction of cotton. Thread mills, once numerous, had been reduced to four. There were also diaper and muslin looms, and a declining calico printing business beside the Avon. There were three breweries for porter, ale and small beer. The brewers were still obliged to use the burgh mills, which they complained was too expensive. There had been four distilleries, then reduced to one, plus the 'manufacture at Bonnyton' which employed 24 men. There were several bakers, making bread "remarkable for its fine colour and delicate taste", but the bakers were also restricted to the burgh mill. There were four corn mills in addition to the burgh mills.

The burgh had the right to levy customs on all cattle crossing the bridge or any part of the Avon, and the revenue of the town, amounting to £400 a year, came mostly from these customs and from the burgh mills. Of the six fairs, the most popular was that of St Magdalene, on 2nd August, but they were not so well attended as they used to be. Poultry was expensive and scarce. Fish was obtained from the loch (eels, pike and perch) and trout from the Avon; coal came from the Bo'ness and Grange collieries. The parish had 58 heritors [landowners], the main ones being Johnston of Straiton, the Earl of Rosebery (who owned vast stretches of West Lothian), the Countess of Dalhousie, the Earl of Hopetoun and Reverend Hamilton of Riccarton - "few of the chief heritors live in the parish. The most ancient is Hamilton of Westport". The town population had been calculated at 2,282. There were 80 or 90 people on the poor roll, mostly strangers, a lot of them Highlanders. There were two inns with post horses and travellers' accommodation. 430 dissenters had been identified, and, like every parish in the country according to these accounts, the 'people [were] in general sober and industrious'. No minister admitted to an unruly flock.

Canal and Railway

In 1790, the Forth and Clyde Canal had been completed, but it did not serve Edinburgh which needed transport routes for its coal and stone and lime supply. In the early 1790s, a movement started for the construction of a canal linking the coalfields and quarries to Edinburgh and Glasgow. The first proposals were put at a public meeting in the Merchants Hall in Edinburgh in January 1793. The surveyors John Ainslie and Robert Whitworth were appointed to work out possible routes, which would have to cross high ground. In 1797, a civil engineer, John Rennie, asked to comment on these routes, submitted yet another route north of the Bathgate Hills. This route would have no locks, and had the advantage of potential passenger traffic through Linlithgow and Falkirk. But the economy was depressed, drained by the Napoleonic wars, and the project was abandoned.

It was revived in 1813, when the price of coal in Edinburgh was very high. Hugh Baird, the engineer of the Forth and Clyde Canal, was asked to draw a plan for a Union Canal, linking the capital to Glasgow via the other canal. Baird estimated the cost at £235,167, with an annual revenue of £52,727, mainly from coal, lime, stone, timber, and iron as well as from passenger traffic. Baird's plan was the subject of violent controversy, not least from those landowners whose estates were on or near the proposed route, as well as to whose coalfields would be accessible. Several plans and routes were debated. The Edinburgh magistrates went into a huff, at the behest, it was said, of the local coal monopolists. A mob broke the windows of the Lord Provost's house, resenting his stand against cheap coal. Baird revised his plan and the Duke of Hamilton, who owned coalfields on the proposed route, joined in the debate. After all the heat, the Union Canal Bill of 1815 was defeated. But the project was revived, Baird reviewed his plan, and the Union Canal Act was eventually passed in 1817. The Act carefully preserved the rights of such landowners as Forbes of Callendar, Duncan of Glenfuir, and Blair of Avontoun to be spared from it. Most importantly, it also preserved the burgh's entitlement to customs duties. A committee was elected with Hugh Baird as engineer and George Moncrieff as clerk. Influential landowners were given substantial sweeteners for the hardship they were going to suffer by contact with nearby navvies digging the canal.

The work was divided into lots, and tenders invited for each lot. The contractors were asked to give 'reasonable preference' to local unemployed men, but men from Ireland and the Highlands were also taken on in great numbers. Among them were two Ulster Catholic labourers, William Burke and William Hare, who, some ten years later, were to find a less strenuous way of making money in the dark closes of Edinburgh. Burke stated that he "came to Scotland to work on the Union Canal and wrought there while it lasted". He worked on the Linlithgow section, living at Polmont and Maddiston. Hare worked at the eastern terminus, Port Hopetoun. Their paths did not cross until much later.

The ethnic mix was a recipe for trouble. Highlanders and Irish men, both victims of British history, were hostile to each other. On one occasion, Irish labourers working in Broxburn drove out some Highlanders, who got some reinforcements the following day, leading to a pitched battle at Winchburgh, with spades and pickaxes as weapons; it was not a pretty sight. There was also a riot in Ratho in 1818. Soldiers usually divided the combatants.

The work was carried out between 1818 and 1822, with the superb aqueducts over the Water of Leith, the Almond and the Avon built to Telford's design. It was complicated by the demands and greed of local landowners, who insisted on a great number of extra drains, bridges and roads. They stood in the way of the easiest route and forced the company to buy them out at ransom prices.

Even in its heyday, following its opening in May 1822, the canal was never a great commercial success. The company was in difficulty from the start; the cost of the aqueducts and the land problems made it worse. The revenue was lower than projected, and prices for goods and passengers had to be reduced. Passengers were attracted by publicity centering on the views from the aqueducts and the 'great speed' of the service. In 1835, 127,000 journeys were made. Competition came from the coach services between Edinburgh, Falkirk and Glasgow. In its heyday, there were six passenger boats a day, and a night service was started. All sorts of attractions were organised to while away the long hours of the journey.

The canal was a good idea which had come far too late. What killed it, of course, was the new railway. After a decade of arguments between vested interests, the Edinburgh and Glasgow line was opened in 1842 (and David O Hill came to Linlithgow in 1845 to take what are believed to be the earliest photographs of a railway station). The canal went into a long decline, traffic ceased in 1933, and it was finally closed in 1965. There it might have remained, but one of the local success stories is its revival, both by British Waterways and the local volunteer group (LUCS) over several decades. The lazy meandering of the canal in Linlithgow is one of the best historical legacies of the burgh, a wonderful amenity and a source of great local contentment.

The New Statistical Account

A report in 1832 sums up the economy of Linlithgow: "A few new houses have been built, but there has not been much increase of the town of late years... the chief manufacture is that of tanning and preparing leather. Some glue is also made, and there are two distilleries and a brewery. There appears to be little or no trade [external trade]". The population was then 3,187, with 316 houses. The New Statistical Account, written by the Reverend Andrew Bell in 1845, adds some details. There was a papermill on the Avon, and the population of Linlithgow Bridge was largely dependent on calico printing. There were two active glue-works and "a number of women, principally unmarried, are engaged in sewing for Glasgow manufacturing houses. This employment can scarcely be termed remunerative for the utmost that a female can earn, working with the utmost diligence from morning to night, is about 6d per day – a most miserable pittance, when we consider the toil of the over-tasked female, who, however, but for this, scanty as it is, would be often entirely destitute. The employments of the operatives are generally healthful, and noway injurious to correct moral habits. A portion of the workmen are, as in every town, dissipated; but this arises from other causes than the nature of their occupation: others, again, are highly intelligent and religious, most favourable specimen of Scottish intellect and piety". The town was not building fast: "The place has an antique air, many of the houses having that aspect of decayed grandeur which testify to the power and opulence of their ancient owners. It is, however, gradually changing in its look of 'venerable old' as modern buildings are usurping the place of these worn-out edifices". The town was lit by gas.

The number of dissenters had grown to 1300; there were two subscription libraries, a newsroom and a society for the purchase and perusal of periodicals. *Dick's Advertiser*, a small monthly sheet printed in Linlithgow, circulated in the county. There were nine friendly societies associated with unincorporated trades set up for the purpose of providing for the sick and old, all of them prosperous and holding considerable property. 140 people were on the poor roll and the prison had been recently upgraded, which brought the minister to approach lyricism: "The prison is well secured and every attention paid to health, and even comfort of the prisoners; each cell is heated with a stove and lighted with gas, regularly cleaned, and as well ventilated as the situation of the prison will admit. Each prisoner, when brought in, is washed and clothed in a prison dress. The diet is excellent, consisting of six ounce of oatmeal made into porridge, for breakfast, with three fourths of a pint of buttermilk. Dinner ox-head broth, four ounce barley, four ounce bread, and a proportion of vegetables, each alternate day, pease-brose, fish and potatoes. Supper the same as breakfast. Provision is also made for the religious instruction of the prisoners, in addition to the services of the chaplain, each cell is provided with a Testament. Mr Alison instructs the male prisoners and his wife the female prisoners. Many of them appear to value the instruction they receive, and some of them make considerable progress". Most writers of Statistical Accounts had their hobby horses, and this was obviously that of Reverend Bell. This spirit of moral improvement was presumably extended to the new workhouse built on the Edinburgh Road in 1856, and demolished in 1969: reports on its operation were usually complimentary.

"One of the most charming features of Edinburgh surroundings is the town and castle of Linlithgow" wrote the German novelist Theodor Fontane in 1858 while on a tour of Scotland. But it was not the town itself which impressed him so much as the Palace, for which he had come prepared with extensive historical knowledge and romantic associations. "The railway station lies at the eastern end of the little town", continued Fontane, "the view that lies before you is as unremarkable as it can be. A sawmill stands opposite the railway station. On three sides it is enclosed by trees and only on the side which faces it is it open and lies before us like a picture in a frame. It interrupts the stillness that reigns all around with its regular rhythms. The mallows, which are in full flower, add the charm of colour to all the rest and enhance the impression of rural peace... From the railway station we turn right towards the town, which actually consists of only a single street. Neither the individual houses nor the situation are on the whole in any way remarkable. It is a little town like a thousand others... these tenement houses, sometimes painted green and sometimes yellow, remind us of our German homeland and not of the towns of England". Fontane, having noted the pastel rendering of the Linlithgow houses, went on to enthuse about the Palace and Queen Margaret's Bower.

A certain *folie de grandeur* runs as a leitmotiv in Linlithgow history: every now and then the Town Council went over the top, digging in its heels in a petulant, stubborn, irrational fashion. It went to court over trifles (a trait shared by many Scottish lairds over the centuries), it pursued judicial actions beyond the point of reason, it carried out grandiose plans which could not be supported by such a small place, it failed to see the passing of the medieval order, it lacked perspective. One such action was the dispute with James Kirkwood. Another was the decision to build the Victoria Halls on the occasion of Queen Victoria's Golden Jubilee. The Hall was built by public subscription, over the site of Brockley's Land, a modest property which had been more in keeping with its surroundings. Portentous, ugly, vast, out of all proportion with the size of the town and of the neighbouring buildings, it soon proved to be a white elephant, epitomising the worst of Victorian taste, immortalising the provost of the time, Andrew Gilmour, and becoming an endless subject of controversy. Another example was the court action against the railway company for the right to charge customs over goods coming through the town. Was there not a series of royal charters confirming their right to charge for goods crossing the Avon into the town? The case went to the Court of Session twice, then to the House of Lords which finally ruled against the council. The burgh was ruined by the legal bills, trying to enforce 14th-century privileges in the age of steam.

Ironically, the line of the canal and of the railway did much to preserve the linear pattern of the town, serving as substitute town walls, containing the old town within its original structure.

Dreamthorp

The burgh had his share of illustrious men, such as Stephen Mitchell, the tobacco lord, James Glen of Longcroft, Professor Sir Charles Wyville Thomson of Bonsyde House, David Waldie who discovered the anaesthetic powers of chloroform, the first Marquess of Linlithgow (the Green Man). But Linlithgow was not blessed with literary talent. It had to content itself with Alexander Smith (?1830-1867) a pattern designer from Glasgow who lived in the town before his premature death. In 1863 he published *Dreamthorp*, which is both the title of a collection of essays and of the first essay. In it he writes under the persona of a retired old man in Dreamthorp: "the children playing in the single straggling street, the mothers knitting at the open doors, the fathers standing about in long white blouses, chatting and smoking; the great tower of the ruined castle rising high in the rosy air, with a whole troop of swallows – by distance made as small as gnats – skimming about its rents and fissures... I had found a home... everything around one is unhurried, quiet, moss-grown, and orderly. Season follows in the track of season, and one year can hardly be distinguished from another... Dreamthorp can boast a respectable antiquity, and in it the trade of the builder is unknown. Ever since I remember not a single stone has been laid on top of another. The castle, now inhabited by jackdaws and starlings, is old; the chapel which adjoins it is older still, and the lake behind it, in which their shadows sleep, is, I suppose, as old as Adam... the houses are old, and remote dates may yet be deciphered on the stone above the doors; the apple-trees are mossed and ancient... every now and then a horse comes staggering along the towing-path, trailing a sleepy barge filled with merchandise. A quiet indolent life these bargemen lead in the summer days... the Dreamthorp people are Dissenters, for the most part; why I could never understand, because dissent implies a certain intellectual effort... here I ripen for the grave". It goes on in this vein at some length. What are we to make of it? Was Linlithgow such an egregiously lethargic place?

Probably not. The writer is having his little joke. Just as the writer's persona is that of an old man rather than the energetic young man he actually was, the place is given the persona which the writer probably assumed would attract his English readers. Linlithgow became a sleepy old village in the Home Counties, the magnificent church a chapel, the Palace a ruined castle, the busy tradesmen idled their lives on their doorsteps, the horses loitered along the canal instead of earning a competitive living for their drivers. Let's forget about Dreamthorp, it was never Linlithgow.

The 20th Century

Most of the writers of the past centuries commenting on the burgh lamented the number of old houses and yearned for or welcomed new ones. And those new houses which displaced beautiful but hopelessly ruinous buildings were welcome and pleasant. This can hardly be said of the developments of the mid-20th century when the Third Statistical Account was written (1965). It saluted the widening of the High Street, the demolition of old properties on the north side between the Cross and the West Port, admitting that the old Spanish Ambassador's House included in the demolition was "regretted by those with a regard for the past". It looked forward to the new housing then at the planning stage. What replaced these old unsanitary beautiful decrepit houses were modern flats out of character with their surroundings, badly built and totally spoiling the homogeneity of the High Street. That they got a design award only added salt to the wound. Some of them have already been demolished, achieving a far shorter lifespan than the structures they replaced.

All the industries and crafts mentioned in the earlier Statistical Accounts have now disappeared, including those, such as the Regent Works and Lochmill papermill, built in the interim. The leather crafts, shoemaking, glue works, distilleries, papermills and calico works have gone. The town is now a very pleasant dormitory town with very little local industry, apart from the significant presence of the electronics firm, Sun Microsystems. Large housing estates have been built on the outskirts, edged out by the restrictive lines of the canal, railway, and loch. In 1974, two conservation areas were drawn in the historical centre of the burgh, putting an end to large-scale architectural vandalism.

Ancient tombstone in the graveyard of St Michael's Parish Church. Also in the well-maintained churchyard is the Livingston Burial Vault of 1668 with its mortsafe.

Palace, Church and Loch

The juxtaposition of Linlithgow Palace, St Michael's Parish Church and Linlithgow Loch is one of the most impressive sights in Scotland, although its tourist potential is, to a large extent, untapped. Set on a high promontory jutting into the loch, the 15th-century palace is the oldest surviving in Scotland, while the adjacent church, with its distinctive modern 'crown', was consecrated in 1242 and is one of the country's finest parish churches.

Linlithgow Loch and Peel

The 102-acre (41-hectare) loch, containing several small islands, is both a recreational resource and a wildlife sanctuary. Fishing and dinghy sailing, the latter mainly by children under expert instruction, are the main water-based activities, while the water and the loch banks are home to large numbers of swans and mallard ducks, plus other species such as tufted duck, pochard, moorhen, coot, great-crested grebe and cormorant, just a few of the 90 which have been identified. The swans are said to have departed from the loch during the period of the palace's occupation by Cromwell's troops, not to return until King Charles II's restoration to the throne.

It is considered possible that crannogs may have been constructed over the loch. The surrounding Peel, a royal park like Holyrood Park in Edinburgh, is an important asset to the town, a venue for the children's Gala Day, and a mecca for day-trippers, many of whom visit Linlithgow just for the pleasant walk around the loch. Below the palace on the loch shore was the Bow Butts where archery was practised, while the Peel was the setting for local cricket matches until, in 1930, the West Lothian County Cricket Association opened its new pitch at Boghall.

Left The gateway and the main entrance to Linlithgow Palace from the graveyard of St Michael's Church. Above the gateway arch can be seen four carved panels representing the orders of knighthood borne by James V - the Golden Fleece, St. Michael, the Garter and the Thistle.

Right Dramatic view of the south range of Linlithgow Palace, St Michael's Church and the town beyond. In the foreground, in the centre of the palace courtyard or Inner Close, can be seen the elaborately carved hexagonal well which dates from around 1538. Reputed to have been set to run with wine on the visit of Bonnie Prince Charlie to Linlithgow, it is similar to the town's Cross Well and its design was copied for the forecourt of the Palace of Holyroodhouse.

Classic view of the palace and church from the south-west. The lochside path on the right had to be reclaimed from the loch in the 1930s, as the owners of the adjacent riggs (or back gardens) refused to sell.

Linlithgow Palace

The first royal residence or manor house at Linlithgow was established on the easily defended loch side site, now occupied by the palace, in the 12th-century reign of David I. In 1301-02, during the occupation of Edward I of England, this became incorporated into a larger fortification designed by James of St George, architect of the great Edwardian castles in North Wales, and including St Michael's Church within its boundaries. After 1314, the military works were demolished on the orders of King Robert the Bruce, and the present palace, with its squared courtyard plan, was started for James I in 1424 and built in five main stages over the next two centuries. Originally, the main entrance was from the east, but, around 1540, it was moved to the south where it has remained. James V was born here on 10th April 1512 and, by the time of the birth of Mary, Queen of Scots in the palace on 8th December 1542, the building would have largely assumed its present form. But decay set in, and, after a roof fall in 1607, the north range was rebuilt in Danish Renaissance style for James VI. In July 1633, King Charles I was the last monarch to stay in the palace, and, around the same time, the Scottish Parliament met here several times.

Between 1650 and 1659, the palace was once again fortified and occupied, this time by Cromwell's troops, the defences consisting of a new stone wall, material for which was obtained by demolishing the town's hospital, school, Town House, manse and any other buildings nearby. These fortifications were removed in 1663. Bonnie Prince Charlie was entertained here in 1745 and, a year later, after having been occupied by soldiers of the Duke of Cumberland, the Palace was gutted by fire and has remained a ruin ever since. Nineteenth-century ideas of conversion into the County Buildings or into a supplementary Register House came to nothing and the building has been in State care since 1874. Ideas for restoration are still discussed and there is abundant documentary and physical evidence of its former appearance and structure. The palace is open to the public and further details can be found in the excellent guidebook produced by Historic Scotland.

Right Looking southwards past the 'utter gret bulwerk' of the palace towards St Michael's Church.

Below The Great Hall or Lion Chamber in the east range of the palace looking towards the magnificent fireplace with its three-part hearth and broad hood. Its former glory was recalled when King George V held court for an hour in 1914, and most recently on the present sovereign's visit to Linlithgow in 1989.

Bottom Right Unusual and imaginative view looking up towards the original (pre 1540) entrance to the palace.

Views of the church and palace from near and far...

Much of Linlithgow's attractiveness stems from its close relationship with the loch, Linlithgow Palace and St Michael's Parish Church. This selection of photographs shows this relationship from various viewpoints in and around the town.

From the northern shore of Linlithgow Loch.

From St Ninian's Road.

From the north-eastern extremity of Linlithgow Loch.

From the foot of Manse Road.

From the access road to Clarendon Farm.

From the eastern corner of the Peel.

From Fiddler's Croft, towards the east end of the loch.

Again from the northern shore of Linlithgow Loch.

From Rosemount Park.

25

St Michael's Parish Church

This impressive cruciform parish church was consecrated in 1242 by David de Bernham, Bishop of St Andrews. It is the second largest church in the Lothians, being 182 feet (55 metres) long and 103 feet (31 metres) across the transepts. It was largely rebuilt after a fire in 1424, initially under the supervision of John French who was buried in the north aisle in 1489, and most of the existing fabric dates from that period. The Lords of the Congregation removed nearly all the pre-Reformation imagery in 1559, and, prior to restoration of the building in 1894-96 by Honeyman and Keppie, the church had become disfigured by high galleries and a towering central pulpit in the chancel. The south transept, where James IV saw the ghost warning of his impending doom at Flodden, has a window with magnificent Gothic tracery and modern stained glass portraying the Pentecost by N Crear McCartney. Until 1821, the church tower was topped by a 15th-century stone crown; this was eventually replaced in 1964 by a controversial structure of bronze-tinted aluminium, designed by Geoffrey Clarke. Within the tower are three bells, namely Alma Maria (Blessed Mary) of 1490, Meg Duncan and St Michael.

The interior of the church is well lit by the large windows at the east end of the chancel. Of particular interest are the timber pulpit adorned with statues of Mary Queen of Scots, Queen Margaret, Queen Victoria and the present Queen Elizabeth, the variety of stained glass and the Burgh War Memorial, built into the east wall of the south aisle and designed by Dr McGregor Chalmers. Ministers have included the Very Rev Dr David Steel during whose time the new crown was added, and the very energetic Rev Ian Paterson who celebrated 25 years at St Michael's in 2002. The church is open to visitors throughout the summer months, and a detailed guidebook is available from the church shop.

St Michael's Church from the palace grounds. The car park is likely to have been the site of the royal stables and the falconers' mews.

The church from the graveyard, showing the south entrance porch with priest's room above.

The car park and palace gatehouse, with the main church doorway on the left, as seen from within the palace. Situated at the top of the Kirkgate, this outer entrance to the palace was built by James V around 1535, as a result of which the main door of the church opened directly into the palace precincts - a bone of contention which brought about three serious, but ultimately unsuccessful, attempts to restrict right of access to the church.

The magnificent nave and chancel of St Michael's Parish Church.

Bronze plaque on the front wall of the Sheriff Courthouse, commemorating the death of the Regent Moray, shot by James Hamilton of Bothwellhaugh in 1570 from Archbishop Hamilton's house, once situated in this vicinity. The plaque (1875) was designed by Sir Noel Paton and engraved by his sister, Mrs Amelia Hill.

Around the Cross

The Cross is the centre of activity in Linlithgow - the natural focal point where the Kirkgate, giving access to the palace and the parish church, meets the High Street. In the words of local historian Bruce Jamieson, "here have been held food sales, livestock auctions, public executions, royal proclamations, witch burnings and aristocratic festivities". Although it has long since lost its traditional Mercat Cross, today it is still the principal venue of the Riding of the Marches and preparatory activities, the Advent Fair, the Renaissance Fair and other community festivities; weather permitting, it is always a pleasant place to sit and watch the world go by. The late Colin McWilliam, architectural historian, has stated that "no other town in Lothian, perhaps not even Edinburgh, has a grander civic focus".

Left The Cross and Kirkgate as seen from high up in Linlithgow Palace, showing the tower of St Michael's Parish Church on the left and the backdrop of Rosemount Park and the Bathgate Hills.

Right A view down the Kirkgate to the Cross, showing the old cottages, their crow-stepped gables and the attractive new paving and lampposts, installed in 1995 by the former West Lothian District Council. The three-storey building at the foot of the street is the original part of Cross House which dates from 1700.

Linlithgow OLD AND NEW

...the Cross Well, made by a one-handed stonemason

The Kirkgate leading up to the Palace Gateway, the cottages of c1700 on the left featuring traditional crow-stepped gables and raised painted margins to their windows. The churchyard retaining wall on the right features a series of plaques recording, with one significant Hanoverian error, the line of succession from Mary, Queen of Scots to our current queen, who celebrated 50 years on the throne in 2002.

Looking up the Kirkgate from the Cross, showing the towers of both St Michael's Parish Church and Town House.

One of the Kirkgate cottages.

30

The Cross showing the Burgh Halls or Town House with the tower of St Michael's Parish Church in the background.

The Cross Well, made by a one-handed stonemason called Robert Gray who is said to have worked with a mallet strapped to the stump of his handless arm. Dating from 1807 and costing 300 guineas, it is said to be an exact copy of a previous well of 1535, rebuilt by John Ritchie of Edinburgh in 1628. It is hexagonal in plan and features cusped flying buttresses, mask-gargoyles and a crowning circular cupola holding a scroll with lion rampant. The water for the original Cross Well came from a wellhead in the present-day Rosemount Park; unfortunately the 19th-century version was not plumbed in!

The Town House (Burgh Halls)

Replacing the original tolbooth demolished on the orders of Oliver Cromwell in 1650 to create an open area around the palace for defensive purposes, the present Town House was built in 1668-70 by John Smith, based on original designs by John Mylne, Master Mason to Charles I and Charles II. The New Statistical Account of 1845 records that the building contained a jail, the sheriff courthouse and the town hall. There was a serious fire in 1847 (some of the resulting stone damage can still be seen) and the building was restored a year later by Thomas Brown. The stone entrance steps, which had been replaced by an iron loggia to give more room for the market, were restored by William Scott in 1906. The Town House and the classical Old County Hall to the rear were combined in 1962 by Rowand Anderson, Kininmonth and Paul to form the present Burgh Halls, and, afterwards, the local tourist information centre was established on the ground floor. The tower has clock faces on three sides and was provided in 1857 by MacKenzie of Glasgow. A steeple and weathervane which had been added in 1678 were not replaced after the 1847 fire. Ambitious plans to upgrade the Burgh Halls were produced in 2001 by consultants commissioned by West Lothian Council. Unfortunately, there has, at the time of writing, been no feedback on comments from local people, nor any further progress towards implementation.

...the 'Green Man', first Marquess of Linlithgow

The 19th-century buildings on the east side of the Cross (also the church and Town House towers if you look carefully), as reflected in the window of the bus office on the opposite side of the High Street. It is unusual, in this day and age, to find an operational bus depot in such a central location! Perhaps a more appropriate use could be found for the site.

The 'Green Man', the 1911 bronze statue of John Hope, sculpted by George Frampton, is now hidden away behind the Burgh Halls, having been relocated from its original site at the Cross in 1970. John Hope, 7th Earl of Hopetoun, was the first Governor-General of Australia (1900-02), and was created first Marquess of Linlithgow in 1902. The area around the statue was previously a curling pond and, before that, the site of the town's Grammar School which possibly originated as a choral school for St Michael's Parish Church. Former pupils include Patrick Hamilton and Henry Forrest, two of the Protestant martyrs who were burnt at the stake in St Andrews, in 1528 and around 1533 respectively. After the 1872 Education Act, the Grammar School became known as the Burgh School. Unfortunately, the building was destroyed by fire in February 1902 and never rebuilt.

The west side of the Cross, showing the flats before their recent refurbishment and, in the background, Cross House which was built by Andrew Craufurd of Lochcote in 1700 and extended to the west by Robert Garner, Commissary of the Royal Forces in Scotland, in the 1760s. The building is category 'A' listed, mainly because of fine internal plaster work, particularly a geometric ceiling in the earlier part of the house and fine rococo plasterwork in the first floor 'Adam Room', featuring swirling foliage, birds and baskets of fruit. During the 18th century, Cross House was also occupied by James Glen, variously Provost of Linlithgow, Governor of South Carolina and Keeper of Linlithgow Palace. In 1988, it was extended through the construction of the Kirk Hall of St Michael's Church, to the designs of William A Cadell Architects.

Court Square looking north with the County Buildings on the right and the police station and Sheriff Courthouse on the left. The County Buildings date from 1935 and were designed in impressive neo-Georgian style by the architect Walker Todd of Dick Peddie and Todd for West Lothian County Council. Notable features include the bay-leaf garland decoration around the top of the window over the front door, and, inside, there is a timber-panelled committee room (with original furnishings), together with fine paintings from the Old County Hall, quality plaster cornices, good timber doors, streamlined metal balustrades to stairs, and green marble and travertine floors in the entrance areas. The lamp standards with decorative bronze lanterns in Court Square and the Provost's lamp at the front are included in the 'listing' of the buildings. The police station also dates from 1935, was designed by the same architect, and replaced an old jail building constructed around 1840. The police were previously based in the same building as the Sheriff Court, and later in Annet House.

Front view of the County Buildings with the Sheriff Courthouse in the background. The courthouse was designed in Tudor style by Brown and Wardrop and completed in 1863, a single-storey cell block being added in 1875. There is a (now rare) fire insurance stone plaque on west elevation, showing a phoenix rising from the ashes.

The Masonic Lodge, next to the Burgh Halls, built on the site of the Fleshmarket in 1905-06 and designed by William Scott.

The late 19th-century offices of the *Linlithgowshire Journal and Gazette* (better known in the town as the *Linlithgow Gazette*) featuring two Dutch gables and decorative rainwater goods - hopper heads with grotesque dragons. The *Linlithgowshire Gazette* was started in 1891 by F Johnston and Company, publishers of the *Falkirk Herald*, and a firm which has since grown to become one of Britain's most important newspaper companies. Next door is the Auld Hole i' th' Wa' public house, one of several in Scotland with similar names, for example in Dumfries, Elgin, Greenock, Musselburgh and Paisley.

The bronze plaque commemorating Dr David Waldie's experiments with anaesthetics in his laboratory above the present Four Marys public house.

5

East High Street

Until the 20th century, nearly everyone in Linlithgow lived and worked in, or very close to, the mile-long High Street. Because of the constraints of the loch to the north and the sloping ground to the south, the town grew as an east-west linear settlement. Its plan layout came to resemble a fish skeleton in the typical style of a Scottish royal burgh, the backbone being the High Street and its continuous lines of buildings. The smaller bones at right angles are represented by the occasional wynd or close, but mainly by the walled back gardens or riggs running up the hill or towards the loch. The High Street's alignment and width evolved in accordance with ground conditions (mainly the steepness of any slopes behind), the functions of the adjoining buildings, and general consensus. Today, its traffic is probably as incessant as when it was the old A9, the main highway from Edinburgh to Falkirk and Stirling, before the M9 bypassed Linlithgow in 1973.

The section of the High Street east of the cross makes up less than a third of its total length, but is, in some ways, the most interesting, both historically and architecturally. Hamilton's Land (photograph opposite) is a remarkable survivor of the late 16th century, while other important ancient buildings such as the Mint and the Greenyards were lost a century ago, reminding us that redevelopment schemes are nothing new! Apart from the 'Loanings' at the west end, this section of the High Street has always been its widest part, but, unlike the Loanings, its trees have gone.

Left View from the steps of the Burgh Halls, showing the wooded, rising ground behind the High Street frontage.

Right Hamilton's Land, late 16th-century tenements with crowsteps and red pantiles, built by the Hamiltons of Pardovan and Humbie and restored by The National Trust for Scotland in 1958 as part of its Little Houses Improvement Scheme. The stone was quarried at Pardovan (like most used in Linlithgow) and, at the top of the left hand building, can be seen a panel with flight holes giving access to the pigeon loft in the attic.

High Street, looking east from the Cross. The prominent turret on the right belongs to the Royal Bank of Scotland. This baronial-style building with gargoyles was originally built in 1859 for the Commercial Bank of Scotland, and the 'CBS' monogram can be seen above the main door. The architect, David Rhind, was so proud of it that he also added his own initials (look for the DR monogram below the angle turret)! On the adjacent site, closer to the camera, was once situated the 16th-century townhouse of the Cornwalls of Bonhard; the family crest from this building still remains, built into the back wall of the present buildings.

The High Street looking west to the Cross where the 'sawn-off' look of the Vennel flats gives such an unsatisfactory visual 'stop' to the view.

The Victoria Hall, named in honour of Queen Victoria's Golden Jubilee, faces an uncertain future. Designed by J Russell Walker and opened by the Earl of Rosebery in 1889, it was used for dances, flower shows and concerts, but was sold by Linlithgow Town Council in 1956 to Caledonian Associated Cinemas for £6,500, as it had become superfluous with the council's purchase of the Old County Hall. It became the Ritz Cinema, seating 620, but bingo crept in, and, by the 1970s, it had become a full-time bingo hall. Latterly it was an amusement arcade, and it has lain empty since the mid 1990s. Before the removal of its turrets and pinnacles in 1956, it had dramatic architectural quality, albeit wildly out of scale with the street. Could this be restored or should the remaining building be demolished and replaced with something more in keeping with its surroundings? Certainly, it is no thing of beauty in its present condition.

Part of the run of well-proportioned 19th-century three-storey tenements at the east end of the High Street; this photograph of numbers 16-18 still shows signs of its use as the Palace Hotel over a century ago. Behind this range of buildings are a number of red-pantiled outbuildings, only now being considered for upgrading and re-use.

Hamilton's Land from across the High Street, contrasted with the modern telephone kiosks outside the Post Office.

Scottish baronial tenement of 1881 at 62-64 High Street, including one of the High Street's many carriage pends. Like Hamilton's Land, it has a doocot - in this instance located in the square turret at the top right of the building. This 2002 picture shows the latest external decor of the hairdressing salon on the ground floor.

Linlithgow OLD AND NEW

...may have functioned as the Royal Mint for a short time

The two photographs above, both taken in 1999, show the changing face of the town's hostelries - here was the transformation of the historic 17th-century Red Lion Inn into the Bar Leo, a real piece of Italy in Linlithgow, Italian contractors and materials being used for the conversion. For many years, the town of Linlithgow lacked a good selection of eating places, but over the past ten years, the east end of the High Street has attracted three quality restaurants, not only the Bar Leo but also Livingston's and the Marynka, both 'Taste of Scotland' establishments. Even the former Red Lion had changed colour over the years - it is marked on Wood's 1820 map as the Golden Lion Inn - perhaps gold paint became too expensive!

The Post Office, an exceptionally well detailed piece of Scots Renaissance architecture but perhaps rather too low a building for its site. Designed by W W Robertson, it was built in 1904 on the site of the Greenyards, a 17th-century crow-stepped building of striking appearance.

The Four Marys public house, well-known for its selection of real ales. The rear part of the building, and its neighbour at 63 High Street, now attractively lime-washed, are 18th-century and were built on an earlier building line. Here was the birthplace in 1813 and laboratory of Dr David Waldie who conducted experiments into the anaesthetic properties of chloroform (later taken up by the much better known Dr James Young Simpson). Commemorating him are a plaque on the frontage, made by R Hope Pinker in 1913, and the "Loving Cup" or Waldie Memorial Cup, drunk from during the Marches celebrations.

Left High Street roofscape and St Michael's Parish Church, looking down over the station approach.

38

High Street roofscape and St Michael's Parish Church from the end of the station platform, with St Michael's Wynd in the foreground. Prior to the arrival of the railway and the canal, St Michael's Wynd led straight up to the hill to the present line of Manse Road. The building with the red pantiles is a former house, about three hundred years old.

St Michael's Well, the most interesting of the town's well-heads, supports an inscribed stone dated 1720 and a winged figure of St Michael with the burgh's other coat of arms. Its waterspout was removed following a traffic accident. In the background, the three-storey Baronial tenement of 1886, with its interesting skyline, originally had a hotel above the shops, but this was converted into flats around 1992. The site of these buildings was previously occupied by 'The Mint', the early 16th-century town house of the Knights Hospitallers of St John of Jerusalem whose Scottish headquarters were at Torphichen. So called because it may have functioned as the Royal Mint for a very short period of time, it consisted of a large blackened tower, together with various arched buildings ranged round two courtyards. There was an impressive hall with an open timber roof and a carved fireplace. Although the replacement 19th-century edifice is of good quality, the Mint buildings, as recorded in drawings and photographs, would have been of exceptional interest today.

Left This three-storey Baronial tenement of 1885 has the carved inscriptions 'St Michael's Place' and 'Hame's Best' carved above its doors. Since this photograph was taken on a cold winter's morning in 1994, Harrison's hardware shop has closed and has effectively been replaced by Linlithgow DIY further west along the High Street. Now, the ground floor of the building accommodates patchwork and quilting specialists.

Linlithgow OLD AND NEW

6

The supermarket in the Regent Centre, operated by Messrs William Low of Dundee until their takeover by Tesco. The slated pyramid-roofed entrance area was added to the building in the mid 1990s.

High and Low Ports

Two of Linlithgow's three original town gates or 'ports' were situated at the east end of the town, beyond the fork in the roads at the eastern extremity of the High Street - firstly the 'Low Port' on the road to Linlithgow's ancient seaport of Blackness and, secondly, the 'High Port' on the higher route to Edinburgh. At some stage, the street name 'Low Port' was changed to the present 'Blackness Road', while, in the late 19th century, High Port and Edinburgh Road were called 'East Port' and 'St Magdalene's Road' respectively.

It is thought that the area between the High and Low Ports was the site of a pre-Reformation chapel dedicated to the Blessed Virgin Mary, one of four such religious establishments apart from St Michael's Church, the others having been St Magdalene's Hospital at Edinburgh Road, St Ninian's Chapel at the West Port, and the Carmelite Friary up Manse Road. The site seems not to have been intensively developed until 1902 when Alfred Nobel, the Swedish inventor, established a factory to make safety fuses, mainly catering for the needs of the now-defunct West Lothian oil-shale industry. In 1908, the factory, known as the Regent Works, was provided with a distinctive red and yellow brick arcaded front with Italianate towers, designed by William Scott. Nobels were incorporated into ICI in 1926. During both World Wars, ammunition was manufactured on the site, but, in 1949, no doubt much to the relief of those living nearby, the product was changed from explosives to pharmaceuticals (including Savlon antiseptic cream). Prior to the transfer of the business to Macclesfield in 1964, 450 were employed. The site was then purchased by a Leeds clothing firm (R E Spence & Co Ltd) and occupied by a variety of firms, including a sheet metal works and a tyre depot, before the buildings were demolished in 1982 and replaced by the present Regent Centre of shops and offices, designed by Robert Hurd and Partners.

The Low Port Centre, a community and outdoor education centre, was sensitively designed for the site in 1987 by the architects Wheeler and Sproson. Featuring a large staircase mural by James Cumming, it offers residential recreational courses including such activities as canoeing, wind surfing, orienteering and 'mountain' biking.

Two views of the east end of the High Street showing, at the top, a general view over the junction towards Low Port Primary School, and, to the right, the Star and Garter Hotel with colourful summer bedding display in the foreground and the railway station behind.

The building now known as the Star and Garter Hotel was constructed around 1760 and is noted on Wood's map of 1820 as the residence of Provost John Boyd. In 1847, it was converted into a hotel and was, for many years, the base of the Linlithgow and Stirlingshire Hunt which had been established in 1797. In the vicinity of the roundabout was the decorative, cast-iron Whitten Fountain, now disappeared into oblivion. The structure was bought by the Town Council with money left by Whitten, Sheriff Clerk of Midlothian for this purpose and for the planting of trees in the eastern section of the High Street. Like the fountain, the trees have disappeared from the scene. Recent attempts by the Linlithgow Civic Trust to persuade West Lothian Council of the merits of restoring such trees to the street have, so far, been unsuccessful.

...playing field may overlie remains of Cromwellian earthwork

Linlithgow OLD AND NEW

Low Port Primary School.

Low Port Primary School

The impressive structure of Low Port Primary School, designed by J Graham Fairley, occupies an attractive site behind a playing field, and backs onto the Peel and Linlithgow Palace. The school was originally opened in 1902 to relocate Linlithgow Academy from its former home at the West Port, now Longcroft Hall, and was extended to the rear in 1930. Clearly much smaller than it is today, the Academy had a distinguished record on the Low Port site until, in 1968, it was, once again, relocated to its present complex at Braehead Road. After the removal of the Academy, the buildings were occupied as a temporary electronics factory by the Signetics International Corporation, prior to the opening of their new factory at the top of Preston Road in 1970, and then as the Architects offices of West Lothian County Council. The new single-stream Low Port Primary School was established in the former Academy buildings in 1973, and, in 2002, the extension of 1930 was replaced by a new 'state-of-the-art extension', under the West Lothian Schools 'PPP'.

The school building is distinguished by traditional Scottish architectural features such as crow-stepped gables and two-part and three-part windows, divided by mullions and transoms. Perhaps the most outstanding are the round towers reminiscent of Holyrood and Falkland Palaces over the former boys' and girls' entrances.

In the grounds of Low Port Primary School is the Low Port Hut, a venue for the After School Club and all kinds of community activity. Here, a children's party is in full swing.

It is thought that the playing field in front of Low Port Primary School may possibly overlie the remains of a Cromwellian earthwork associated with the defence of Linlithgow Palace between 1650 and 1659. Be that as it may, this green sward is a great asset to the school, and is well used for school sports, for example the sports day on 1st June 1999 depicted in the two photographs above.

The new extension to Low Port Primary School, under construction by Morrison for Alpha Schools Ltd in April 2002 as part of the West Lothian Schools PPP ('Public Private Partnership'). Its architects were RMJM who also designed the new Scottish Parliament building in Edinburgh, and, in the 1960s, tower blocks in Glasgow's Gorbals. Within four months, it was complete and ready for the new school session, providing bright and attractive accommodation on two levels and allowing integration of the whole school into the same building. Although the interior is widely admired, concerns have been expressed about the over-use of fashionable, untreated, red cedar cladding on the outside walls. This, and the window designs, seem discordant with the original school building and its location adjacent to the Peel. It is perhaps ironic that the work was carried out before the removal of similar wooden cladding from the Council's 1960s West Port flats for ease of maintenance.

The school garden at Low Port Primary School.

43

The roofscape of the former St Magdalene's Distillery and villas in Back Station Road, as seen from the Union Canal towpath.

7 The Eastern Fringes

The eastern edges of Linlithgow were not subject to large-scale expansion until the late 1960s since when the whole area between Baron's Hill and Burghmuir has been built up with private housing. The resulting Springfield housing estate is, to some extent, physically cut off from the rest of the town and some of the later housing, particularly on the south-east fringes, has lost any kind of 'Scottish' feel. Although, as elsewhere in the town, old industrial and commercial sites have been converted or redeveloped for housing, the area has also seen the creation of a major new source of employment - Sun Microsystems at Blackness Road.

In contrast to Springfield, the vicinity of Edinburgh Road has seen relatively little development with the result that, in this quarter, the countryside still comes close to the centre of the town. All of these eastern fringes are now, however, threatened by large-scale urban expansion. Should this take place, it would be essential that there are accompanying benefits to the community of Linlithgow such as better access to the M9, traffic relief for the High Street, adequate schools and the refurbishment of the Burgh Halls and the Victoria Hall, to name but a few worthwhile projects.

St Michael's RC Church and Presbytery, dating from 1887 and designed in the Gothic style by the renowned church architects, Pugin and Pugin. The church was enlarged in 1893 and internally modernised by J A Coia in 1952, but the proposed 64-foot tower was unfortunately never built. Immediately adjoining is the presbytery or priest's house, overlooking Blackness Road, while, also in the church grounds, is the non-denominational Laetare Centre, Scotland's only International Youth Hostel, which was started by the then parish priest, Father McGovern, 60 years ago. During the Second World War, this was the base of a Polish ambulance brigade. From 1892 until 1963, St Joseph's Primary School was also located in the church grounds.

Above Looking down over the railway to Baron's Hill, Madderfield Mews and the station and Tesco car parks. Atop Baron's Hill (which is a 'drumlin', a rounded hill created during the last Ice Age) is the mansion of the same name, dating from 1913 and designed by W Scott in Scottish Arts and Crafts style. The houses of Madderfield Mews (madder was a root crop used to make dyes) on the right were constructed in the mid 1990s by Ogilvie Homes of Stirling on the site of an old whisky bond. Along their northern edge runs the Bell's Burn on its roundabout way to Linlithgow Loch under the front of the Tesco supermarket and via the west side of the Low Port Centre and the back boundary of Low Port Primary School. Capstan Walk, which gives pedestrian access to Springfield alongside the burn, recalls the 'rope walk' which was once located there.

Right Provost Road, looking south towards the old St Magdalene's Distillery. It is no longer a through route except on Marches Day, Gala Day and other special occasions when the pend through to Edinburgh Road is opened up for westbound traffic.

...whisky, ploughs and computer servers

The top two pictures on this page show the four-storey west malting barn of 1880, attached to the double kiln with its distinctive pair of pagoda roofs, before and after the conversion of the malting barn into flats by R & G Homes of Dunfermline in 2002. Shown in the picture to the left are the East Barns (with a similar kiln) which were converted into flats in 1989 to the designs of Cooper Design Associates. In subsequent years, the rest of the site, sloping up to the canal, was developed with townhouses and flats by Laing Homes, later taken over by Persimmon Homes.

Edinburgh Road looking north from the Union Canal aqueduct, showing large recently-constructed bungalows on the left and the Morrison Bowmore bonded warehouses, constructed around 1960 and recently reclad, in the background. Leading off to the right is Maidlands, a small housing estate which lies on the site of the St Magdalene Engineering Works where Alexander Newlands and Sons made farm machinery, mainly ploughs, for a century until closure in 1983.

St Magdalene's Distillery

The distillery for the manufacture of single malt whisky was established on the Edinburgh Road in 1834, the business having previously been established at Bonnytoun Farm in 1800. The canalside location allowed enhanced access to supplies of coal and coke, also peat from the Slamannan area. Provost Adam Dawson of Bonnytoun House was an owner of the business, and, after A and J Dawson Ltd went into liquidation in 1912, the concern was taken over by the Distillers Company. Before its closure in 1983, over 60 people were employed at the distillery. The name derives from the pre-Reformation St Magdalene's Hospital, first mentioned in 1335, which once stood in this vicinity, possibly under the East Barns. This was a refuge for poor or ill people, especially lepers, while the name suggests that repentant prostitutes may also at one time have found shelter. The name Pilgrim's Hill, a quarter of a mile to the east, may be related to this religious foundation. Closer to St Magdalene's in more recent times was St Peter's Convent, converted from the villa of Greenpark in the late 19th century, now demolished and the site occupied by a petrol filling station. Up the hill to the south-east, immediately to the north-east of the present St Michael's Hospital, was Linlithgow Poorhouse, set up in 1856, and demolished in 1969.

The large, low-set factory of Sun Microsystems Ltd in its well-landscaped surroundings on Blackness Road. The original factory, dating from 1990, was designed by the Parr Partnership, with a later extension by the Holmes Partnership. As with most modern electronics factories, the exact nature of the goods manufactured are something of a mystery to the general populace, but, in this case, the main product is computer servers. The plant is Sun's only manufacturing base outside America, and a large, previously moth-balled extension was opened in October 2002, increasing the number of employees and contractors on site to nearly 1,000.

Right Bonnytoun House, possibly designed by Thomas Hamilton around 1840, as seen from Blackness Road. This Tudor-style villa, with its fine classical interior, was built for Adam Dawson, the proprietor of St Magdalene's Distillery and provost at the time of the reconstruction of the Linlithgow Town House after the 1847 fire. Accordingly, a pediment at the entrance to its walled garden is said to have come from the pre-conflagration Town House.

Springfield from the towpath of the Union Canal.

Springfield Road, looking east, showing the first phase of the Wimpey development.

Springfield

The Springfield housing estate, almost a township in its own right, was mainly constructed by Wimpey Homes, over the period from the late 1960s to around 1985. In 1969, prices on this estate were quoted at 'from £4295'. At the same time, the eastern slopes of Baron's Hill (and the site of the former Boghall Territorial Army Centre) were being developed with a range of villas, chalets and bungalows by D B Gunn (Builders) Ltd of Edinburgh. An innovative feature of this development was (and is) 'the luxury of oil-fired central heating', supplied by means of fuel piped underground from a central oil storage tank at the top of the hill and then metered at each house. Since the oil crisis of the 1970s, higher prices have greatly reduced the use of the system.

From the 1960s, Wimpey Homes, in common with other (British) national house builders, tended to produce 'Scottish' versions of their house-types, featuring, for example, greater use of harling rather than facing brick. After 1985, however, this practice largely ceased and, for about fifteen years, brick houses, indistinguishable from others being built anywhere else in the United Kingdom, were built in large numbers, and this is reflected in the style of the houses by other builders which finished the Springfield development. Now, elsewhere in the town and in most parts of the country, there is a welcome trend back to reflecting Scottish tradition in speculative housing developments, at least in the middle and upper sectors of the market.

Following the completion of the developments at Sheriffs Park and Bailielands by Beazer Homes and others around 1990, further development in the area was undertaken by Cala Homes, directly off Blackness Road. This upmarket development was carried out in two phases (Grange View and Grange Knowe) around 1995-1997.

Bonnytoun Nursery in the year 2000. This nursery school, along with the adjacent 'open-plan' two-stream Springfield Primary School with its 'community wing', is centrally situated within the Springfield neighbourhood. Opened around 1980, these were the very first 'facilities' provided specifically to serve the expanding local population.

It was not until around 1990 that Springfield was provided with its first shop units, in a single row at the (fairly) central roundabout. Market forces have dictated that only the one conventional local shop (the Spar) seems to be viable at this location, a mile distant from the High Street. This takes up most of the floorspace, the remaining units currently being given over to a Chinese carryout and a small dental surgery. Surplus land adjacent to the shops was taken up by a small development of townhouses by Miller Homes in 1992 which brings some welcome building height to the area - the character of this community focal point is perhaps not ideal in that, contrary to the tradition of having greater building height and density in town, village or neighbourhood centres, the largely two-storey Springfield decreases to single-storey in and around the shops.

Luckily, Springfield is relatively well located for sports facilities, having grown up next to the ground of the West Lothian County Cricket Association and close to the bowling green, tennis courts and other attractions of the Linlithgow Sports Club at Boghall. Additionally, the Kingsfield Golf Driving Range, portrayed above, and with twelve floodlit covered bays, has recently been established on ex-farmland a short distance to the east.

The number inscription of the Manse Road canal bridge. The corners under the north side of the bridge are marked by deep grooves gouged by the tow ropes of the horse-drawn canal barges.

8 Around the Canal and Railway Station

Linlithgow has always been an important centre of communications, but the local topography has dictated the east-west emphasis already described. Although having status as the county town of West Lothian, the burgh has always had poor road links to the southern part of the county, partly because of the steep gradients over the Bathgate Hills, but mainly because of the greater demands for east-west communications between the major Scottish towns and cities. The completion of the Union Canal and the Edinburgh and Glasgow Railway, in 1822 and 1842 respectively, reinforced the east-west emphasis and stemmed the natural growth of the town to the south. Ancient routes, such as St Michael's Wynd/Manse Road, were blocked and diverted while the tops of many of the riggs or High Street back gardens were chopped off by the railway. But, for many years, Linlithgow exploited relatively little benefit from the canal and the railway. The canal's commercial viability was comparatively short-lived and, for some reason, it was not until around 1960 that Linlithgow was 'discovered' as a dormitory town for railway commuters. And it was not until even more recently that the leisure potential of the beautiful Union Canal was officially recognised.

Left Diesel multiple units 'stationary' at Linlithgow in 1999, showing trains in ScotRail and Strathclyde Passenger Transport livery. The distinctive red roofs in the background are those of the flats at Regent Square.

Middle Right The canal basin, looking east to Bridge No 43.

Bottom Right The view west from Bridge No 43. Behind the trees on the left is the classical, early 19th-century Canal House, the home of canal engineer Hugh Baird. Part of Canal Terrace to the right was built as the Union Canal Inn in 1840 and restored as cottages in the mid 1970s by Gordon Duncan Somerville.

The Union Canal Basin with the former stables, now a museum and tearoom operated by the Linlithgow Union Canal Society (LUCS), in the background. The basin, cottages and stables all date from around 1820.

The Union Canal

Started in 1818 and opened in May 1822, the Union Canal linked the centre of Edinburgh to the Forth and Clyde Canal at Falkirk. Its length of 31.5 miles (50.7 kilometres) was engineered on the level by Hugh Baird, except for a flight of locks at the Falkirk end. When completed, it was 5 feet (1.5 metres) deep, 37 feet (11.3 metres) wide and 20 feet (6.1 metres) wide at the bottom. Although its commercial viability was effectively ended by the opening of the Edinburgh and Glasgow Railway in February 1842, it limped on until August 1965 when it was closed to all traffic. Immediately, short-sighted roads authorities started to replace bridges with culverts, including one at Preston Road, Linlithgow, making through navigation impossible. As a result of public pressure, the canal was re-opened for recreational purposes in 1973, and in 1990 the Preston Road culvert was changed back to a bridge, even with 'swan' warning signs, curiosities which unfortunately quickly disappeared. The greatest advance has taken place over the last few years with the completion of the Millennium Link project, part funded by the Lottery, which has restored the Forth and Clyde and Union Canals to through navigation. In May 2002, on her Golden Jubilee tour, Her Majesty the Queen officially inaugurated the Falkirk Wheel, the spectacular rotating boat lift linking the two canals.

The canal boat 'St Magdalene' on the Avon Aqueduct, a spectacular twelve-arched structure, 810 feet (247 metres) long and 86 feet (26 metres) high, three miles west of the Linlithgow Canal Basin. The water is held in by a cast-iron trough. Resident engineer Hugh Baird and the famous Thomas Telford worked together on the design and construction of this and the other two main aqueducts on the Union Canal. Weekend afternoon boat trips to the aqueduct are run by the Linlithgow Union Canal Society (LUCS) throughout the summer months. LUCS was formed in 1975 and, as well as running the museum, tea room and trip boats 'Victoria' and 'St Magdalene', actively encourages canal restoration/improvement, produces publications and organises a canal rally (fun for all the family!) every August. It is entirely a voluntary organisation, and all activities are conducted by unpaid members.

View looking westwards from the top of Bridge No 46 with the ten-year-old Braehead Park housing plot development, promoted by the former West Lothian District Council, on the right. The bridges over the Union Canal are numbered consecutively, working westwards from Edinburgh.

A cyclist proceeds eastwards towards the Canal Basin.

The pleasant surroundings of houses in Deanburn Road, looking east from Bridge No 46. This particular bridge is little used nowadays, apparently having lost its original purpose.

Linlithgow Railway Station

Despite alterations in the late Victorian period, in 1964-65, and again in 1985, this remains one of the best preserved original through stations completed by the Edinburgh and Glasgow Railway Company in 1842. Featuring massive stone retaining walls and one of the first subways on a Scottish railway, it is thought to have been designed by John Miller. The waiting room off the eastbound platform features a large mural by Mary-Louise Coulouris depicting the annual Linlithgow Marches procession. Now the twelfth busiest station in Scotland with 6,000 return journeys per weekday, it has recently been comprehensively refurbished and restored by Railtrack.

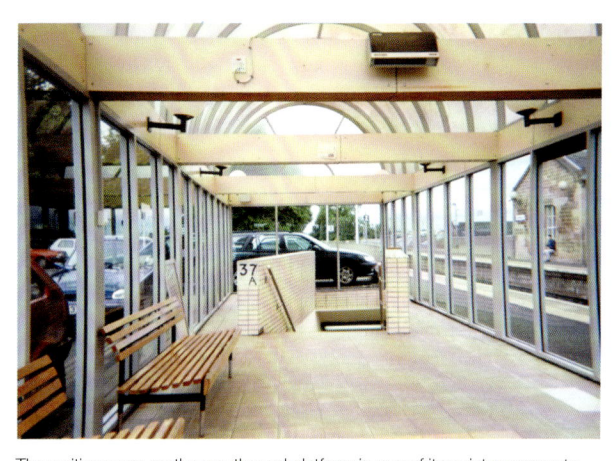

The waiting room on the westbound platform in one of its quieter moments.

General view of the station on a Sunday.

The attractively-restored canopy on the eastbound platform, showing the doors of the new station lift.

53

...string courses designed to stop the ingress of rats

The upper part of the pedestrians-only Station Road, as seen from the foot of Manse Road, with Low Port Primary School and Airngath Hill in the background. On top of the hill is a monument commemorating Brigadier Hon Adrian Hope who was killed in India in 1858. The rather incongruous flat-roofed house on the right occupies the site of the former Linlithgow East United Presbyterian Church, built in 1807 and disused in 1917 (see the account of St Ninian's Craigmailen Church in Section 13).

Opposite The magnificent single birch tree in the garden of Wellbank, a mid 19th-century cottage at Strawberry Bank/Station Road.

The Learmonth Gardens, given to the burgh in 1916 in memory of Alexander Learmonth, Provost of Linlithgow between 1802 and 1807, provide a neat and colourful setting for the 16th-century Ross Doocot. Built for the Barons Ross of Halkhead to provide fresh pigeon meat, probably on the rigg of their High Street town house (now very likely occupied by the Royal Bank), the doocot contains 370 nest boxes and was last repaired in 1991. Its projecting string courses were designed, not only for decoration, but to stop the ingress of rats.

Impressive monkey puzzle trees at Back Station Road with, in the background, the sadly decaying remains of the west malting barns of the St Magdalene's Distillery, prior to their recent refurbishment as flats.

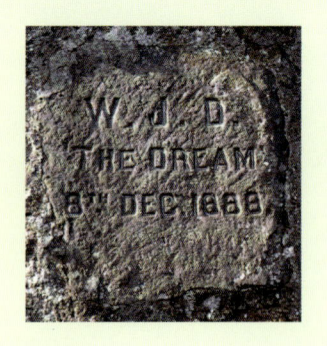

The stone plaque commemorating a horse's leap over a high wall near the top of Friars Brae. According to the 1856 Ordnance Survey Map, there was an 'old quarry' on the opposite side of the road at this point; this had been covered over by 1895.

The Southern Suburbs

Despite the barriers imposed by the construction of the Union Canal and the Edinburgh and Glasgow Railway (or perhaps because of them), the uphill slopes to the south of the High Street became the fashionable location for prosperous lawyers and merchants to build their villas, firstly in classical style in Royal Terrace and then increasingly on larger, more isolated sites further up the hill. Apart from the inter-war development of council houses on the lower ground next to Preston Road, surprisingly little development followed until around 1960 when James Harrison and Company (Builders) Ltd constructed a substantial new development of mainly detached private houses at the top of Friars Brae, previously a quiet cul-de-sac petering out into a countryside footpath. This was quickly followed by substantial numbers of houses at Clarendon Road (Miller Homes, c1963-1969), Oatlands Park and Laverock Park (Bradley Homes, 1969 onwards), Deanburn (Weir Construction Ltd, c1970), Riccarton Road (c1972), and Priory Road (Varney Homes (Scotland) Ltd/Bovis Homes, 1973 onwards).

The whole of the remaining area out to the Dark Entry was built up by around 1990, at first by the development of the large detached villas at Deacons Court by James Harrison and Company (Builders) Ltd and then mainly by Walker Homes. Also established at the top of Preston Road in 1970 was the electronics (integrated circuits) factory of the Signetics International Corporation of California, later, as from 1983, occupied by Racal (radar systems) and now being promoted by present owners Thales for residential development. This apart, the mature trees and stone walls associated with the earlier development of isolated mansions and villas, together with the good views to the Ochils and the Perthshire mountains, give the residents of much of Linlithgow's southern outskirts an excellent quality of environment.

A well-mannered classical house in Royal Terrace, dating from the early 19th century. As stated in *West Lothian - An Illustrated Architectural Guide*, 'the retention of the original glazing bars demonstrates the importance of these proportions'. The construction of the houses in Royal Terrace had already begun before the coming of the railway in its deep cutting in 1842 - hence the high retaining walls - but the passage of the trains did not deter further building, resulting in the wide range of good quality house types, ranging in style from classical to Victorian.

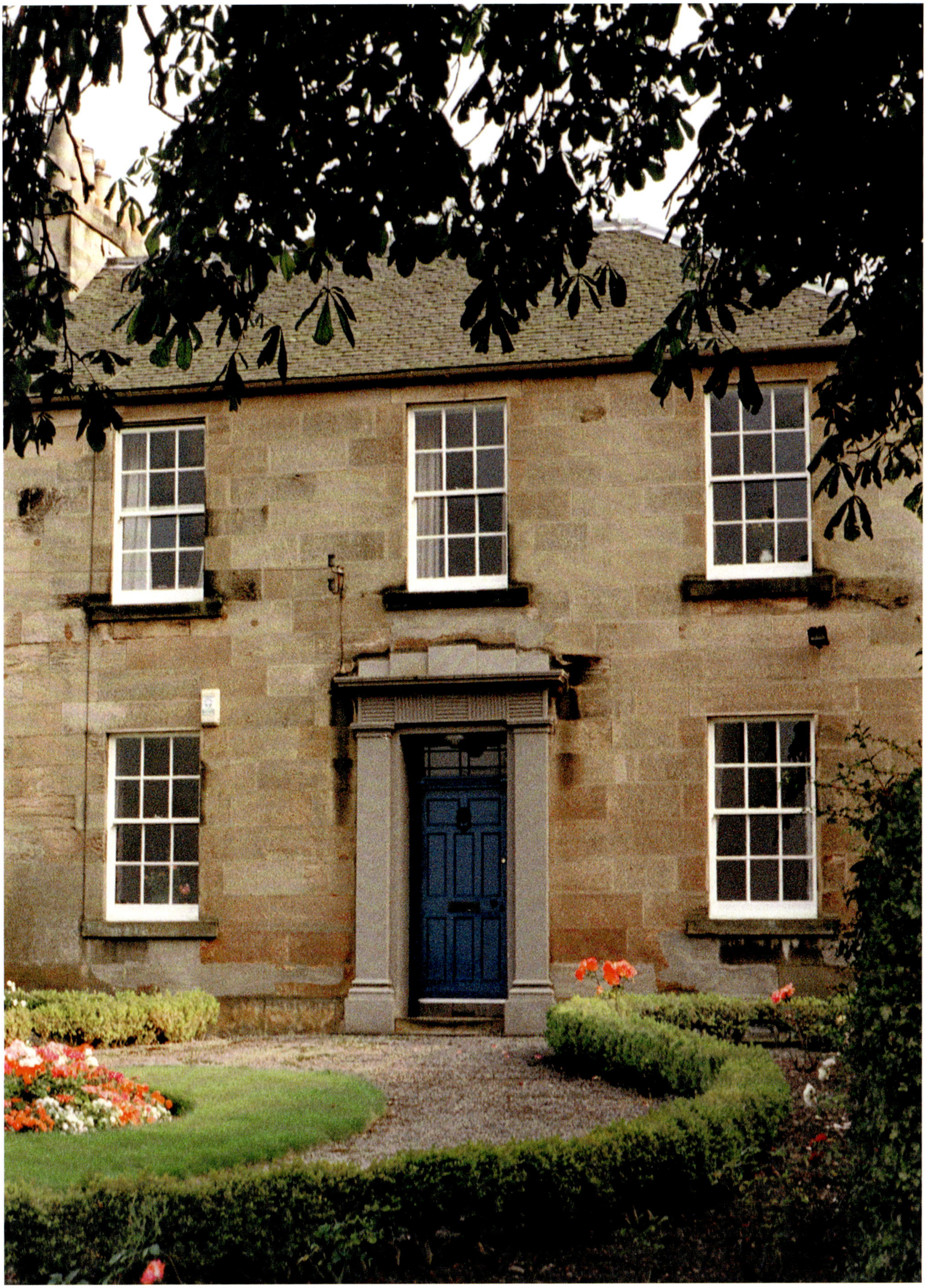

...site of the tithe barn of the Carmelite Friary

The east end of Royal Terrace, showing the height of the retaining wall supporting the street, in relation to the buildings behind. Particularly notable is the early 20th-century, three-storey front extension in Arts and Crafts style to the right of the picture. After the foot of Friars Brae, the street changes its name to Strawberry Bank. Here (under numbers 18-20) is thought to be the site of the tithe barn of the town's pre-Reformation Carmelite Friary.

Attractive Victorian cottage in Union Road (facing Royal Terrace across the railway) complete with original decorative porch, dormer windows and octagonal chimney pots.

Good inter-war council housing and attractive play park off Preston Road. Flowering cherry trees beautify this park in the springtime.

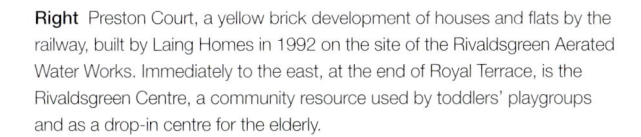

Right Preston Court, a yellow brick development of houses and flats by the railway, built by Laing Homes in 1992 on the site of the Rivaldsgreen Aerated Water Works. Immediately to the east, at the end of Royal Terrace, is the Rivaldsgreen Centre, a community resource used by toddlers' playgroups and as a drop-in centre for the elderly.

A new Barratt private housing development at Barkhill Road, developed in 2000 on the site of the joinery works of Smith and Frater, previously occupied by the Rivaldsgreen Tan Works. The name 'Barkhill Road' is derived from the storage of tree bark which was used in the tanning process.

Good attempt at sympathetic modern infill development in Union Road.

59

...the girls-only school had fees of two pence per week

Attractive scene by the Union Canal, off Friars Brae.

Mrs Douglas' Cottage School, now Douglas Cottage, which was built in 1826 on the south bank of the (then) newly-constructed Union Canal - a late Georgian building in the Tudor style. The girls-only school, which had fees of two pence per week, was accommodated in one-half of the building, while the other half was the schoolhouse. In 1884, by which time the school was under the control of the Burgh School Board, it is recorded as catering for 48 pupils. Five years later, the educational use of the property ceased on the formation of an endowment trust (the Douglas School Endowment).

The fountainhead of the Cross Well in Rosemount Park, known as the Friars' Well because it served the Carmelite Friary further up the hill. Dedicated to the Virgin Mary and founded around 1401, the friary grew from a chapel of 1290, but was dismantled soon after the Reformation - no doubt its stones can be found in quite a few of Linlithgow's present-day buildings! Archaeological digs over the past 100 years have revealed evidence of a substantial church, cloisters, chapter house, latrine, refectory and graveyard (as well as Neolithic and other prehistoric remains). In recent years, the foundations have been laid bare for public view, with footpath access from both Rosemount Park and Manse Road.

Victorian semi-detached villas with decorative ironwork in the mature landscape of Friars Brae. Opposite is the long drive to Rivaldsgreen House, an early 19th-century Tudor revival villa, subdivided into four apartments in 1978.

In a hundred years' time, hardly any of today's modern housing is likely to have survived unaltered as have the 19th-century examples on this page. Already, this property built by James Harrison and Company (Builders) Ltd in Friars Way is one of very few of the early 1960s houses in the area still retaining its original appearance.

The rustic lane linking Rosemount Park to Friars Brae. Rosemount House, an early 19th-century two-storey house with classical features, was the first (surviving) building in this area, followed by Mrs Douglas' Cottage School in 1826.

Shoemakers Way, an ancient right of way between Friars Brae and Preston Road.

Clarendon Farm and the adjacent mews development of 1991 by Adamson Homes.

Clarendon House, one of the largest mansions on Linlithgow's southern outskirts. The original house was built for William Millar around 1820, the bay windows were added around 1845, and a large extension in 1875 for new owner J Miller Richard included the three-storey Italianate tower. In the 1950s, it became a nursing home. It has been greatly extended in recent years and is now a day centre. Other notable buildings in Manse Road include Glebe House of 1801 (the former St Michael's Manse), and Nether Parkley, an 1881 villa with classical details, designed by Wardrop and Reid. Rockville alone has so far succumbed to housing in its grounds, in 1982 by Cala Homes.

Carved pediment (from the Golden Cross Tavern), the preservation of which was the only concession to the past in the former Linlithgow Town Council's redevelopment of the north side of the High Street, west of the Cross.

10

The Vennel

The 1967 redevelopment of the area west of the Cross, although ambitious, represented probably one of the worst losses of historic townscape in Scotland. The flat-roofed replacements for the ancient stone buildings which once lined the High Street have not stood the test of time and are generally disliked by the townspeople. The shop units are poorly designed, typically featuring entrance steps (awkward for disabled people) and stretches of blank front wall and lacking purpose-built fascias for shop names. Recent opportunities to restore some kind of traditional character to the area have been lost, despite protests from Linlithgow Civic Trust and the West Lothian History and Amenity Society.

A few years ago, the block nearest to the Cross was refurbished in 'modern' style, partly to save money and partly in deference to 'expert' opinion. The refurbishment of the remainder of the buildings is now planned by West Lothian Council, in partnership with Cruden Estates, in yet another variation of the modern style which respects neither the original design of the flats nor the surrounding Conservation Area. Although residents in the flats will, at least, soon have a very welcome respite from the effects of dampness and other problems caused by bad design, how long will it be before the whole lot has to be demolished?

Left Vennel shopfronts.

Opposite Maturing trees and colourful summer floral displays help to soften the harshness of the architecture. In this photograph can be seen a great asset to the town - the recently extended public library (formerly, in part, the Bank of Scotland before it migrated to the Regent Centre). The pedestrian way running north from this point has been named Guyancourt Vennel after Linlithgow's French twin town, an appropriate name as 'Vennel', a traditional Scottish name for a side street or lane, has a French derivation. The Guyancourt Vennel runs in a similar direction, but a little to the east of, the original 'Vennel', a narrow lane linking the High Street (opposite the foot of Dog Well Wynd) to the loch. Another narrow lane or close, which linked the Cross to the lochside, was called the 'Watergate'- perhaps the manner of its redevelopment was Linlithgow's scandal of the 1960s!

63

Linlithgow Town Council took pride in the fact that, in the words of the 1971 Official Guide, the "new town centre and shopping precinct... is reckoned to be the largest undertaken by any authority of this size". Indeed, it is true that the town's municipal house-building activities in the 1960s were concentrated almost exclusively on redevelopment of older parts of the town, while the large-scale construction of owner-occupied housing took hold around the outskirts.

The Vennel redevelopment was designed by Rowand Anderson, Kininmonth and Paul, architects, for the Town Council. Although the design is often criticised, the Council should be given credit for having promoted a bespoke design for the site, rather than standard off-the-peg house types which could, arguably, have been even less suitable. The scheme originally consisted of 90 flats, a variety of shop units, a bank, a double-deck car park, plus a public library, health clinic and public conveniences. As with many modern-style developments, the design was more popular with the architectural establishment than the general populace, and the Linlithgow Comprehensive Development Area (CDA), as it was officially known, received a Saltire Housing Award in 1969.

These five-storey blocks were designed with spaces underneath to allow glimpses of the loch from the High Street.

An example of a shopfront making the best of the rather bleak High Street facade of the western block, with hand painted fascia board.

The western side of the 'Guyancourt Vennel' with Todd the Fishmonger's shop; in the background are the premises now used by the 'Power Station' (a very commendable church-based youth initiative) and Thomas Grieve & Son, the appropriately-named firm of funeral undertakers.

Close-up of the Todd the Cod's 'side' window, facing the High Street.

Although at the expense of losing the traditional, continuous High Street frontage, one of the bonuses of the Vennel redevelopment was to open up views of the loch, previously completely hidden from the main street. Trees and greenery were introduced to a stretch of the High Street formerly much narrower than now, and the lochside flats were built on the site of the town's gasworks (which were not one of the most attractive aspects of old Linlithgow!).

In principle, Richard Jaques and Charles McKean may be correct in their opinion, as expressed in *West Lothian - An Illustrated Architectural Guide*, that the Vennel redevelopment "was extraordinarily ambitious in trying to recapture the quality of a major burgh rather than the large shoemaking village it had become", but equally true is the general view that the design and layout of the scheme was extraordinarily unsympathetic to the history and townscape of Linlithgow, as voiced in the words of William F. Hendrie: "To the horror of the townsfolk" were built "these three and four storey monstrosities". Unfortunately, some of the architectural arrogance of the 1960s is now back in fashion which perhaps explains why the most recent and proposed refurbishments have not and will not, contrary to what was done over ten years ago in the vicinity of the Health Centre, make any attempt to fit in with the traditional townscape of the ancient Royal Burgh!

...built on the site of the town's gasworks

View down to the loch from the High Street, opposite St Peter's Episcopal Church. Here the buildings rise to six storeys.

Linlithgow OLD AND NEW

...where Robert Burns joined the local Masonic Lodge in 1787

General view eastwards along the High Street, showing the contrast between the original varied frontage (much dating from the early 19th century) which remains on the right and the relatively monolithic form of the 1960s redevelopment on the left.

Along the present Vennel frontage, there was formerly a near continuous line of two, three and four storey buildings, similar to those remaining in the High Street. Of particular importance were the late medieval, four-storey Spanish and French Ambassadors' houses with fine ceilings and woodwork, situated opposite the present-day Sheriff Courthouse. These were a reminder of the days, in this case the reign of Mary, Queen of Scots, when representatives of foreign countries reputedly required a Linlithgow base to have easy access to Scottish kings and queens.

Facing the Cross were the quaintly named Cunzie Neuk public house and the Golden Cross Tavern, the third-floor attic room of which was said to have been where Robert Burns joined the local Masonic Lodge in 1787. Sections of painted wooden ceiling from this room, which dates from around 1700, have been restored and are on display in Linlithgow's museum at Annet House.

Right The brae up to the Cross, showing the contrast between the stark white of the newly-refurbished Vennel flats and the warm colour of the sandstone in the background.

The colourful flower tubs and street trees do much to soften the stark outlines of the Vennel flats and shops during the summer months. The new look proposed for these particular buildings opposite Annet House is awaited with interest.

General view of the recently refurbished block nearest to the Cross, with the tower and 'crown of thorns' of St Michael's Parish Church just showing in the left background.

This representation of Linlithgow's principal historic buildings, fixed to the library wall, is a memorial to the late and greatly respected Jimmy McGinley, a larger-than-life councillor and one-time convener of West Lothian District Council.

Traditional chemist's sign in the High Street (outside what is now a health food shop).

West of the Sheriff Court

West of Linlithgow Cross, the High Street drops in height, past the Sheriff Courthouse. At the foot of the brae, the street opens out with the Vennel flats on the right and the curvilinear traditional building frontage on the left. Prior to the Vennel redevelopment, this was consistently the narrowest section of the High Street, and, although the Vennel has its faults, the set-back of its building line at least allows better appreciation of the remaining built heritage on the south side. Although only a few of these buildings have outstanding architectural quality, they have considerable 'group value' as they follow the street's irregular building line.

As well as recording some of these traditional frontages, this section explores Dog Well Wynd and Lion Well Wynd, leading up, parallel with the stone rigg boundaries, to the incredibly narrow Union Road alongside the main railway line. Union Road follows, at least in part, the back of the ancient town wall which still retains some 17th-century doorways.

Opposite Looking down Lion Well Wynd towards Linlithgow Loch. Lion Well Wynd is the steepest and perhaps the most interesting of Linlithgow's uphill wynds, said to have been opened around 1750, although the picturesque grouping of houses dates only from the 19th century. Several of the buildings in the wynd were restored by William A Cadell Architects in 1979-80. In particular, the restoration work on number 19, with its forestair, received a Saltire Award in 1979. The stone walls on both sides are also 'listed' as of architectural/historic interest, as are the retaining walls up to the railway footbridge at the top.

Left Dog Well Wynd, looking down towards the High Street. The 'Spires' housing development immediately on the right was constructed on the site of the Linlithgow West United Presbyterian Church which had been built in 1834 to replace an earlier church displaced by the railway, and had become redundant in 1954 when a union of congregations brought about the present St. Ninian's Craigmailen Church (for fuller history, see Section 13). The Scout Hall further down the wynd on the left was once McAlpine's shoe factory.

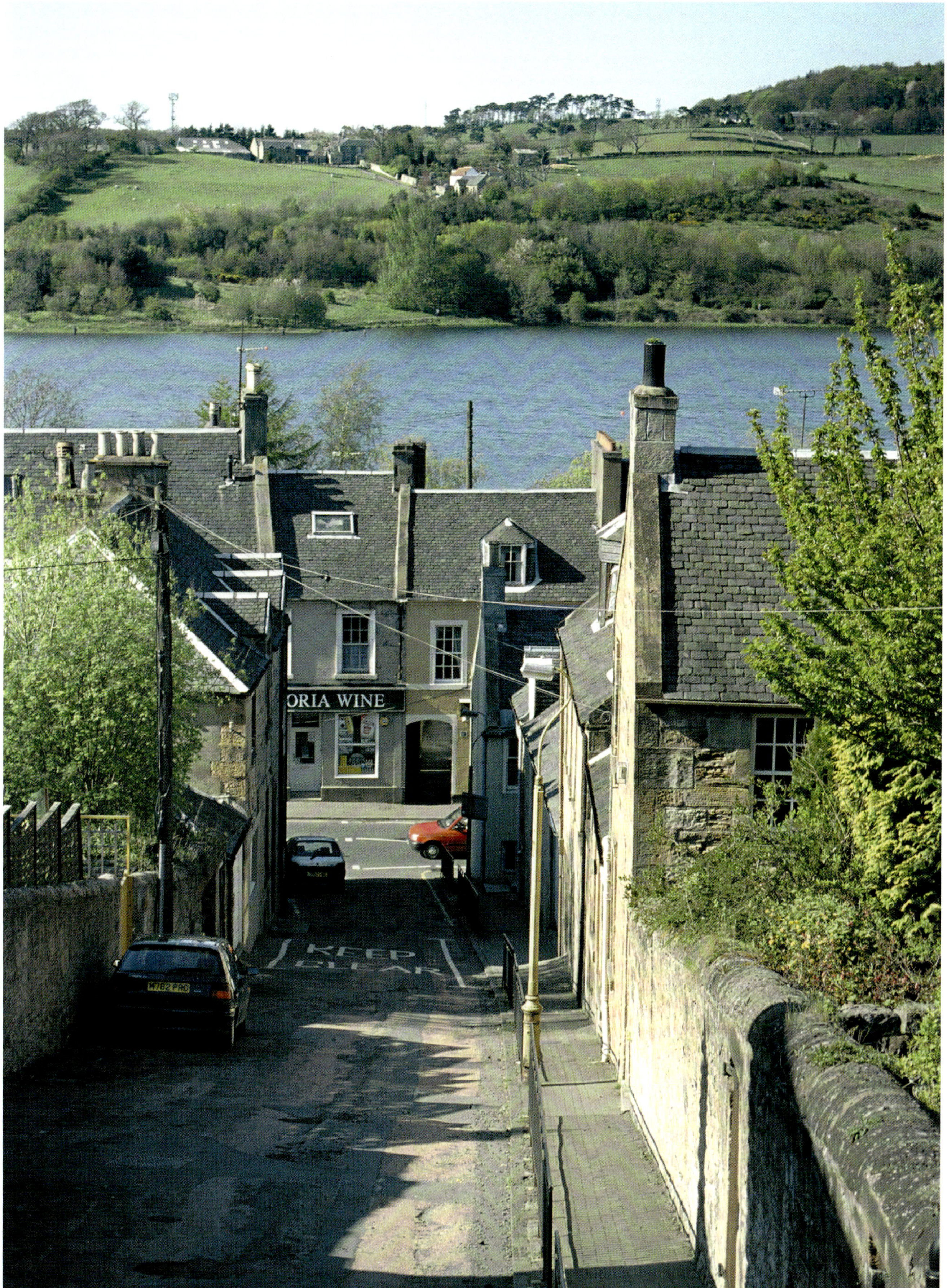
ORIA WINE
KEEP
CLEAR

...Annet House, local museum and heritage centre

General view of the buildings at the foot of Dog Well Wynd. The 200-year-old red-pantiled, three-storey tenement on the left was restored in 1989, while the Football and Cricketers Arms (formerly the Dogwell Tavern) across the wynd occupies buildings of a similar age. An interesting feature of this pub is the original etched glass window of a footballer, facing on to Dog Well Wynd.

Early 19th-century building containing a craft shop (subsequently converted into a children's book shop in 2001) with the backdrop of the mature trees at the Sheriff Court.

Shoemakers' Land, an early 19th-century Georgian house at 123-127 High Street, restored by Linlithgow Town Council just before its unfortunate abolition in 1975. As indicated by the carved armorial plaque high up on the building, the property once belonged to Shoemakers' Guild, reflecting the former importance of the leather trade as a staple industry of the town.

St Peter's Episcopal Church, in the Byzantine style, tucked away behind the High Street's building line. Previously dedicated to St Mildred, the building was completed in 1928 to the designs of Dick Peddie and Todd. The church door is flanked by columns with carved Celtic capitals depicting the Four Evangelists and, inside, a plaque records that George Henry Somerset Walpole, Bishop of Edinburgh, assisted the establishment of the church in memory of his wife, Mildred.

Welcome to worship at the Gospel Hall in Union Road.

Annet House (right), an 18th-century merchant's house, used for a time as a public library, and converted into a local museum and heritage centre in 1991 by the Linlithgow Heritage Trust. A new statue of Mary, Queen of Scots (left), provided by public subscription in memory of Tom McGowran, eminent newspaperman and lover of Linlithgow, and sculpted by Alan Herriot, was unveiled in the recently restored back garden or rigg in 2002.

The 18th-century wellhead of the New Well. Behind the wellhead is A & P Cabrelli's chip and ice cream shop, a long-established Linlithgow institution.

12

West High Street

The only stretch of the West High Street relatively unspoiled by 20th-century redevelopment extends from near the foot of Lion Well Wynd to the Water Yett. Here are the 'Loanings', shown in the top photograph opposite, where the mature trees add to the attractiveness of the scene. A longstanding gap site at this point was eventually developed for Stuart House, the Procurator Fiscal's office, in the 1980s. In the same decade, another gap site to the west, which had been earmarked for a cinema, was infilled by Brae Court, a sheltered housing scheme for elderly people provided by the Bield Housing Association.

West of the Water Yett is another part of the Linlithgow central area redevelopment scheme - the third and final phase. The design and construction of this phase must have been of particularly poor quality, as it was the first to undergo refurbishment, in 1989, less than 20 years after its construction! Although the finished result is far from ideal for its location within a historic conservation area, at least the slated and red tiled, pitched roofs look much better than the flat-roofed originals. (As stated elsewhere, the other similar structures in the area will retain their flat roofs as architectural fashion and economy dictate that they are once again acceptable.) Central to this phase of the redevelopment was a supermarket operated by the Bo'ness Co-operative Society; this property was converted into the Linlithgow Health Centre in 1989.

Left These well grouped and scaled houses in New Well Wynd, stepped up the hill, were designed for Linlithgow Town Council in the 1950s by Rowand Anderson, Kininmonth and Paul. New Well Wynd itself was first created in 1795. In the background can be seen St. John's Evangelical Church, built in 1840 as a Congregational Chapel for the princely sum of £700.

Opposite Top The 'Loanings', looking east.

Right The Swan Tavern at the corner with Whitten Lane; the building, in common with most others in this section of the High Street, dates from the early 19th century.

Far Right The Crown Arms at 177-179 High Street, formerly known as the Masonic Arms.

73

Linlithgow OLD AND NEW

...colourful glazed panels depicting palace and viaduct

Three views of the butcher's shop of T D Anderson at 165 High Street, the lower two (the left is more recent) showing the exterior of the mid 19th-century building and its shop front at the foot of Lion Well Wynd. Of particular interest here is the century-old timber shop gate. The interior decoration, as illustrated in the top photograph, was designed and created by John Duncan of Glasgow in 1912 and features white tiled walls with colourful glazed panels depicting Linlithgow Palace and the Linlithgow Bridge viaduct of the Edinburgh and Glasgow Railway. Along the top is an attractive frieze, while, on the ceiling, are original meat hooks. Completing the scene, taken in October 1999, are Mr George Smith, the displays of goods for sale and contemporary explanatory posters.

The W L Morrison Shoe Shop at 213-215 High Street is the sole remaining business connected with Linlithgow's traditional leather and shoemaking trade. Morrison's is a long-established firm which, until the 1950s, still made shoes to order in their factory across the road on the site now occupied by the Health Centre. The factory was dedicated to St Anne, the patron saint of shoemakers. The firm has occupied its present shop since 1922, housed in a building erected in 1844. Of architectural interest are the double panelled doors with glazed and etched upper panels, the wrought-iron shop gate and the carved wooden display platforms in the shop windows, inscribed 'W L Morrison'. The photographs show Miss Margaret Morrison at the shop door and attending to customers; also the office desk featuring both an old-fashioned typewriter, with, in the background, a slightly more modern microwave oven!

...in the 18th century, there were 17 tanneries

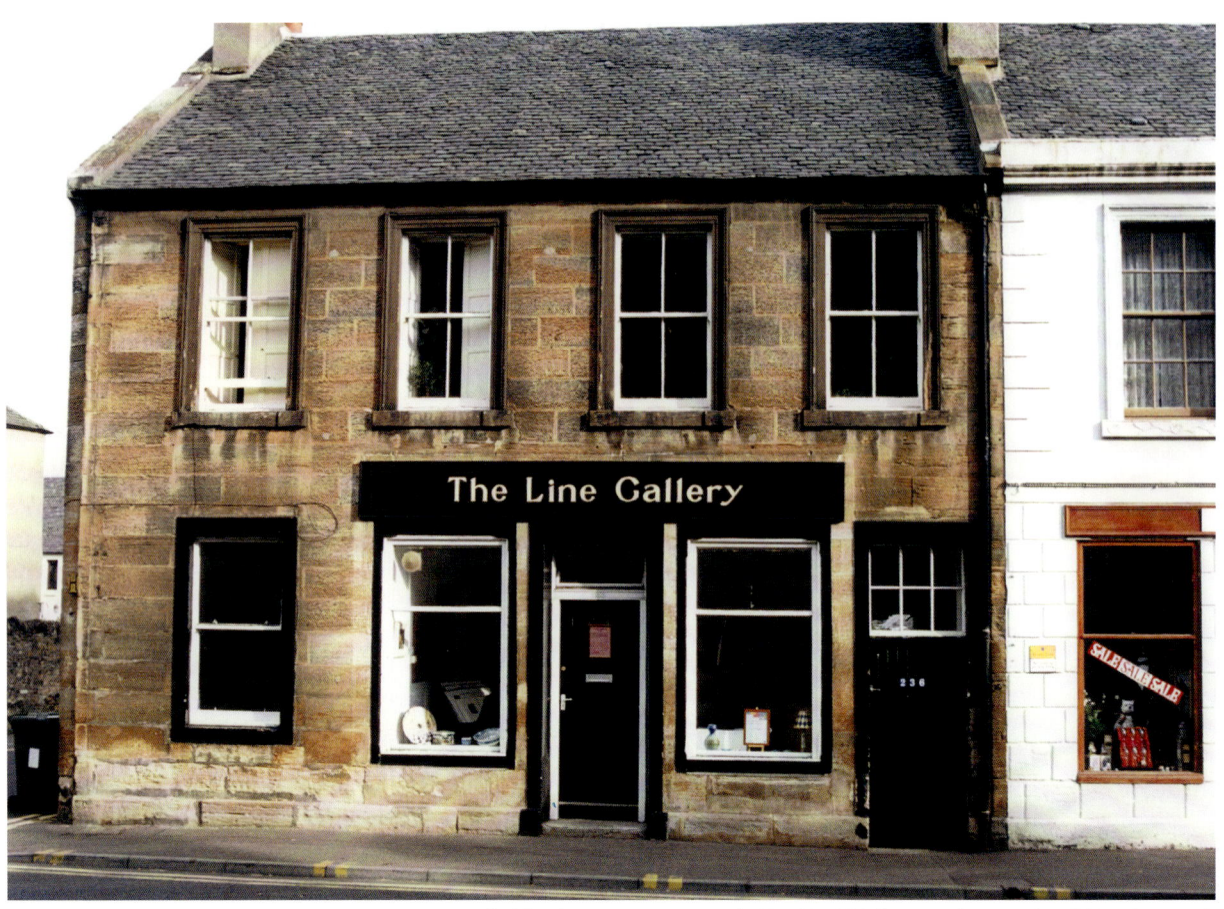

The photographs across these two pages portray a selection of building frontages along the north side of the High Street, working east from Whitten Lane and starting (above) with the early 19th-century Line Gallery building at the street corner.

The former Baird Hall (1863), now a dwellinghouse. The building was designed by Brown and Wardrop and was the gift of Miss Jessie Baird. For many years, it was used for both Catholic church services (the RC parish was then known as St Joseph's) and education. In 1888, the services were transferred to the new St Michael's RC Church in Blackness Road. The Baird Hall remained as a school until 1892 when the new St Joseph's School was completed next to the church. Subsequently, the building was used as hall accommodation by St Michael's *Parish* Church, until the latter's acquisition of Cross House.

Early 19th-century building, directly opposite the foot of Lion Well Wynd. The general arrangement of doors and windows and the retention of the upstairs twelve-pane windows in their classical surrounds, gives the composition a certain homely elegance and symmetry.

The premises of Oliphant's the Bakers at 216-218 High Street. The family business has occupied this same mid 19th-century building since 1856.

212 High Street, a classical early 19th-century building with fanlight, Doric doorway and coach pend. To the rear is an ivy-clad, pantiled former tannery of similar date which is 'listed' because of its importance as a surviving remnant of the 18th- and 19th-century Linlithgow leather trade. It is recorded that, in the 18th century, there were 17 tanneries in the town along with 12 skinneries and 18 currying establishments while, in the mid 19th century, the leather industry employed over 300 men and women. Water from Linlithgow Loch was utilised for the tanning vats, and this explains the former concentration of leather works on the north side of the western portion of the High Street.

Left Lindisfarne, a beautifully-proportioned classical villa, facing Union Road and the railway from behind its retaining wall. Dating from around 1845, it was acquired in 1850 as the manse for the Linlithgow West United Presbyterian Church.

The north-west corner of the Linlithgow Health Centre, originally built as a supermarket by the Bo'ness Co-operative Society. The projecting window feature adds interest to an otherwise dull loch side elevation.

Left The popular lochside children's playground with the St Ninian's Way flats behind. The two flat-roofed blocks in the background were demolished in April 2002, to be replaced by private flats for sale by Cruden Estates. The layout of the new car park to the west of the playground retains part of the old rigg boundaries running down to the loch.

Black Bitch plaque (greyhound chained to an oak tree) on the council tenements at the corner of High Street and Preston Road.

13

Around the West Port

The West Port was the western gateway to the Royal Burgh of Linlithgow, removed around 1800. Prior to the Reformation, this was also the location of St Ninian's Chapel, the precise location of which is uncertain. The hostelries in this area are said to have been established to cater for travellers who were left outside the town gate after it had been locked for the night. The large, open areas were originally drying greens and the West Port area was where the town's present primary and secondary schools originated. West of the loch and the steep slopes south of the High Street, the West Port was, and is, a natural route centre with long-established roads to Bathgate, Lanark, Falkirk and Bo'ness. During the 20th century, the road junctions to north and south were considerably widened through the demolition of old property, but in 2002 the carriageways were narrowed once again as part of an environmental improvement scheme carried out by West Lothian Council. This scheme was controversial, not because of the quality of the work proposed, but because of the lack of traffic lights which, although much desired by local people, were considered unnecessary by traffic consultants.

The vicinity of the West Port contains a considerable variety of housing, ranging from West Port House (now containing the oldest remaining residential accommodation in Linlithgow) to the Edwardian Ashley Hall, and from the Scottish vernacular council housing at the corner of Preston Road to the 1960s flat-roofed flats opposite. To the north are the Bield Housing Association's second development in Linlithgow, the fire station, the Linlithgow Bowling Club, and inter-war municipal housing in Philip Avenue (also leading to two private developments of the 1960s). Yet further north, close to the M9, are the Linlithgow Nursing Home and a recent development of large family houses by Persimmon Homes. Westwards along Falkirk Road are impressive stone-built villas, the first large-scale private housing development in the town at Highfield (Weir Construction Ltd, 1959 onwards), and subsequent housing including Lennox Gardens (Barratt Homes).

Left The smartly maintained West Port Hotel. The hotel has been formed over the years through the alteration of a terrace of old buildings, but the best preserved in the row is the early 19th-century house at the corner with Philip Avenue.

Opposite Crisp traditional detail on the strongly Scottish vernacular tenements built by Linlithgow Town Council in the 1930s (see page 84).

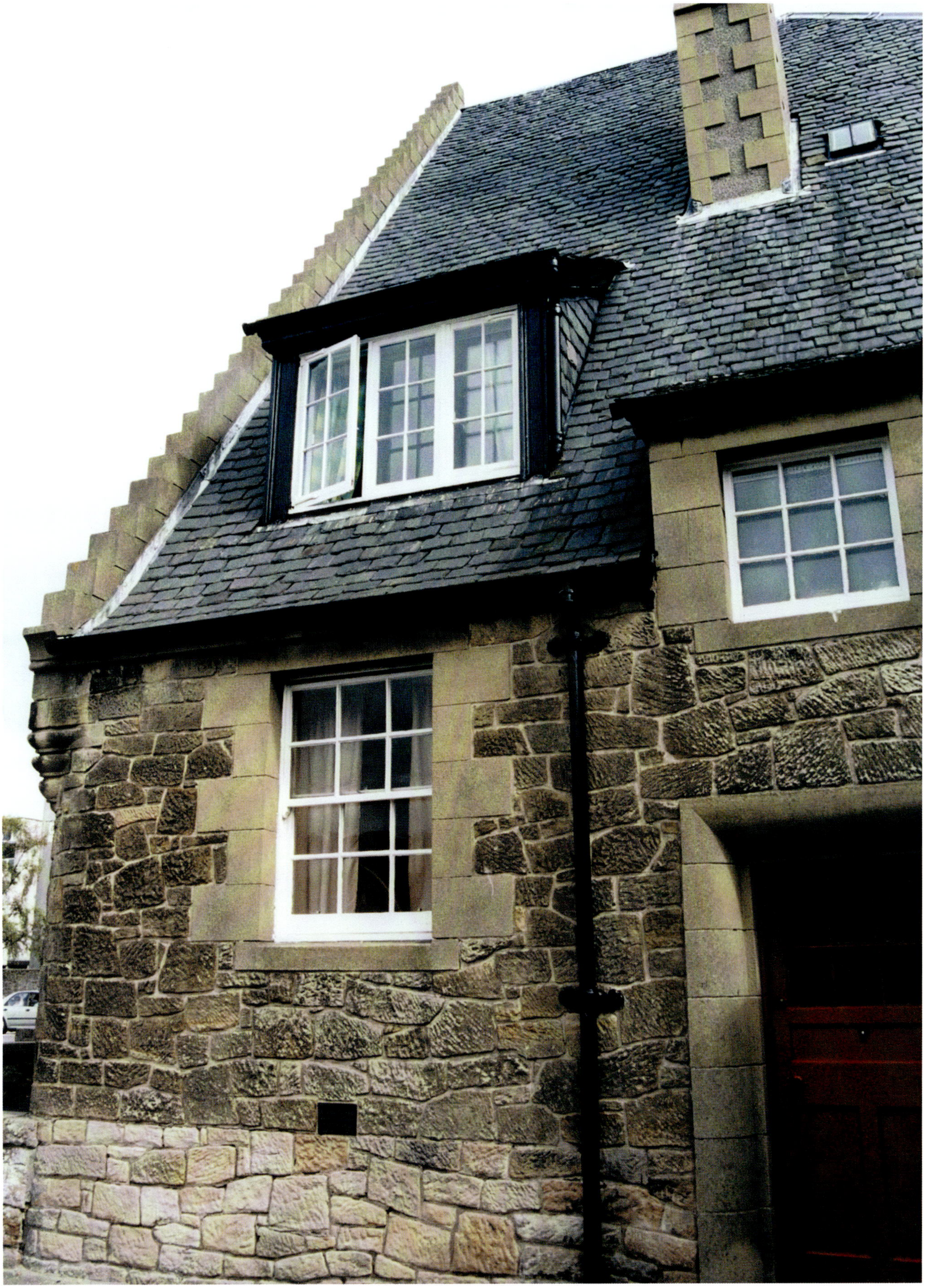

Linlithgow OLD AND NEW

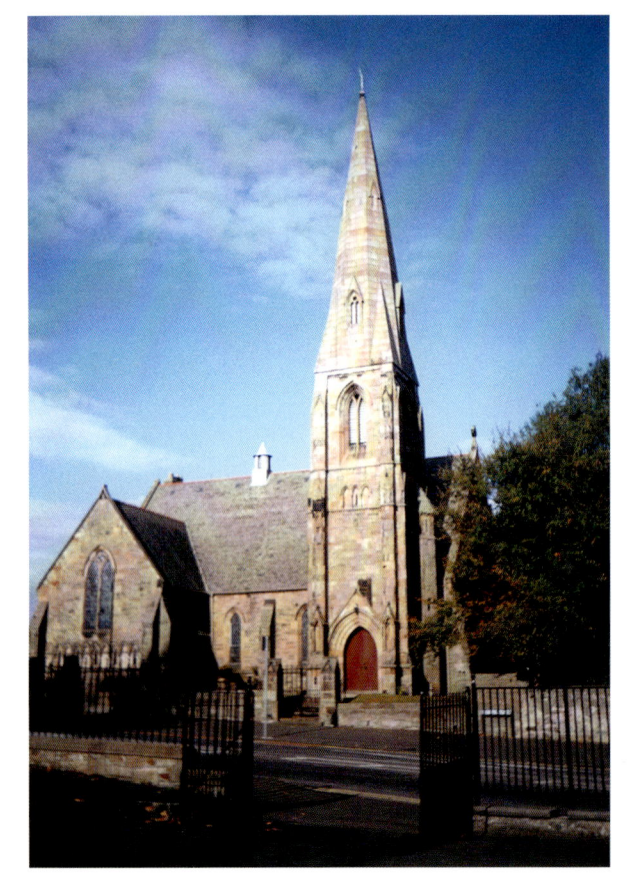

...the term 'Black Bitch' must seem very politically-incorrect

Above General view of the West Port area (prior to the 2002 roadworks), looking westwards to Falkirk Road. This vicinity has since been greatly improved through the introduction of new paving and ornamental lampposts and through the removal of the high kerb-side railings.

Left The Gothic-styled St Ninian's Craigmailen Church with its broach spire, a prominent local landmark, and dating from 1874. The building features a hammerbeam roof and was extended to form a new south aisle and a semi-octagonal hall in 1901. It was built as the Linlithgow Free Church, replacing an 1844 building, later a school, on the opposite side of Falkirk Road. In 1900, on the union of the Free and United Presbyterian (UP) Churches, it became known as the High United Free (UF) Church (of the town's two former UP churches, the West at Dog Well Wynd became the Trinity UF Church, and the East at the top of Station Road continued as the East UF Church). In 1917, the East and Trinity UF Churches united with the name Craigmailen (reflecting the original foundation of a dissenting church in the hills to the south in 1743), using Trinity Church as the place of worship; and, in 1929, on re-unification with the Church of Scotland, the High UF Church was renamed St Ninian's, named after a pre-Reformation chapel which once stood at the West Port. Finally, in 1954, the two ex-UF churches united, becoming St Ninian's Craigmailen.

The church has stained glass windows in memory of Thomas Chalmers and of Jane Dougal by her husband, Robert Mickel of Rivaldsgreen House. Thomas Chalmers was a paper maker who, in 1866, bought the Lochmill papermill which had been established in 1855 by Alex Cowan and Sons of Penicuik. He lived in Longcroft House, a mid-19th-century villa thought to have been designed by David Bryce (see also the section on Linlithgow Bridge). The Lochmill papermill was eventually taken over and closed in the late 1980s by the Inveresk Paper Company Ltd.

Longcroft Hall, built in the mid 19th century. In 1894, it became the first Linlithgow Academy, a fee-paying secondary school. The property now belongs to St Ninian's Craigmailen Church. The area in front, now used for car parking, was the 19th-century Horse Market.

The West Port in autumn, looking east. In the distance is the (claimed) descendant of the celebrated Katie Wearie's Tree, originally blown down in 1911. A replacement sapling taken from it was felled in 1978; a further replacement sapling from that second tree survives today. Below the original tree was Paul's Well. The stretch of road in the foreground was closed to traffic and landscaped in 2002.

Apart from the West Port Hotel, the Black Bitch public house is the only remaining hostelry at the West Port. It is housed in two adjoining buildings, both of which are two centuries old. The western part was heightened later in the 19th century with a mansard roof and dormers. Without knowledge of Linlithgow's history and traditions, the term 'Black Bitch' for a native of the town must seem very politically-incorrect in today's world!

The former West Port Annexe of Linlithgow Primary School. Its playground, recently the venue for the annual 'Street Fair', was the location of the original Linlithgow Public School building (demolished, 1972) which started off in 1843 as Linlithgow Free Church, the predecessor of the present St Ninian's Craigmailen Parish Church. From 1844 until 1872 when it was placed under School Board management, the church building was also used as a Free Church School. The remaining building, shown in the photographs above and below, and nicknamed 'Colditz' by its more recent pupils, was built in 1903 and has an impressive central assembly hall with a wooden beamed roof. Now that replacement school accommodation has been provided at Linlithgow Bridge, the future of this building may be uncertain. It is to be hoped that the structure can be retained and that any new development in the playground does full justice to its prominent location.

Interval at the West Port Annexe, 1999.

81

...prefabs still remain, cunningly disguised

Ashley Hall, an Edwardian villa in Arts and Crafts style, converted to housing for the elderly (Abbeyfield Linlithgow Society) in 1986 by William A Cadell, architects. New housing has been constructed in the grounds.

Above and Below Attractive residential environments near the West Port, rich with mature garden landscapes and the textures of stone, slate and harling.

A handsome bowed stair window, Ashley Hall.

Prefabs were originally built as temporary housing immediately after the Second World War at a time of building material shortages. Fifty years later, however, all of Linlithgow's prefabs, such as these examples at Hamilton Park, still remain, cunningly disguised by the former Linlithgow Town Council as attractive little bungalows! As well as the eight at Hamilton Road, there are four in Preston Road and 28 in Preston Park. Not so long-lived were the prefabs at Kettilstoun Road, Linlithgow Bridge - their sites were redeveloped by West Lothian County Council in the 1960s.

West Port House

West Port House (above) is a three-storey laird's town house occupying a prominent position at the west end of the High Street. The identity of the builder of a previous version of the house on the site is not recorded, but it is known that it was acquired by the Hamilton family after the Reformation and completed in much its present form by James Hamilton of Silvertonhill in 1600. It was restored and converted into flats by William A Cadell, Architects in 1990, ensuring its continued status as Linlithgow's oldest property occupied for residential purposes. It towers over its diminutive neighbour (right) thanks to the lowering of this part of the High Street (and the removal of the West Port gateway) around 1800.

The early 18th-century single-storey and attic cottage at 293 High Street (right) features a pantiled roof and crow-stepped gables. Restored in recent years by Thom Pollock, it was once the residence of George Hay Dick, Printer, Bookseller and Stationer, who published *Dick's Monthly Advertiser*, a local newspaper in the middle of the 19th century. Immediately to the east was a group of 17th-century houses known as Beinn Castle Brae, gable end to the road with pantiled roofs and forestairs. These houses were demolished by Linlithgow Town Council in 1930 to make way for the entrance to the new council houses in St John's Avenue. The new housing site itself was occupied by a brewery in 1856 and a coach works in 1895.

...sensitivity to architectural tradition went seriously out of fashion

'Vernacular' of the 1930s

Tenements in strong Scottish style, dating from 1937, at the corner of High Street and Preston Road, designed by the architect William Scott for Linlithgow Town Council. Such sensitivity to architectural tradition went seriously out of fashion by the 1960s and was not a conspicuous feature of later High Street redevelopments! Note the dramatic 'cat-slide' roofs, crowstepped gables and 'swept' dormers and the unusual view of the St Ninian's Craigmailen spire from behind the buildings. The importance of retaining details such as window astragals on buildings of such quality cannot be over-emphasised, and is recogised by the 'listing' of both blocks as of architectural/historic interest, category 'B'.

'Modernism' of the 1960s

The 1968 redevelopment between High Street and St Ninian's Way, east of the road to Bo'ness, has not stood the test of time and, by the turn of the millennium, needed complete refurbishment. The picture at top left shows the general scene, looking east along the High Street to a subsequent development, originally of particularly poor quality but which received pitched roofs to stop the ingress of water around 1990. The blocks in the foreground are the subject of a refurbishment scheme by Cruden Estates, covering both these and the Vennel flats, and including retention of the flat roofs, much to the irritation of the townsfolk. Whether this is because the architectural fads of the 1960s are back in fashion amongst the design fraternity, or whether it is due to an unwillingness to devote sufficient funds to the job, is a good question. At the very least, the opportunity to correct past mistakes is being lost.

In connection with the refurbishment of the flats, West Lothian Council made available to Cruden Estates the site of the two blocks of flats at St Ninian's Way, shown in the three lower photographs on the left, which were taken just before their demolition in April, 2002. Within weeks, Cruden had started on its replacement block of 34 flats, those overlooking the loch receiving balconies in contrast to the removal of the same feature, noted for residents' floral and Christmas displays, on the council flats facing the High Street. Going too are the interesting textures of the existing natural materials (see photograph, top right) which, albeit not all suitable for the site, are perhaps preferable to the bland replacement white drydash rendering and plastic window frames which would not be permitted by the council on private property elsewhere in the historic town centre!

Linlithgow Academy.

14

South West Linlithgow

Most of Linlithgow's early post-war expansion took place in a south-westerly direction, south of the railway, and west of Preston Road. Along Braehead Road, the town council created a new suburb consisting of both traditionally-built houses and Swedish semi-detached timber villas. There was very little private house-building at that time in Linlithgow, indeed it is likely that only 9 houses were built for owner-occupation between the start of World War I and the mid 1950s. In these days, prior to the town's 'discovery' as an attractive environment for commuters, the town's housing provision catered primarily for the indigenous population. After the development of the Braehead housing scheme, the Linlithgow Town Council turned its attention to central area redevelopment and no public-sector housing development has since taken place on 'greenfield' sites. In fact, very little housing for social renting has been constructed in Linlithgow over the past quarter century and it is becoming increasingly difficult for people of limited means to obtain a house in the town. Perhaps there is a need for the establishment of a housing association to cater for local need, but always there is the problem of the constraints imposed by limited educational capacities, traffic congestion, etc.

Larger-scale housing development in the south-west quarter of Linlithgow resumed in the 1980s with the construction of the owner-occupied houses at Avontoun Park. As the building site had been a sand and gravel quarry, later infilled with the remains of Linlithgow's demolished historic buildings, it was necessary for the houses to be founded on concrete 'rafts'. During the 1990s, the whole area between Avontoun Park and the Union Canal was developed for detached private housing, first by Balfour Beatty and latterly by Persimmon Homes.

This sector of the town has seen a concentration of educational and sports facilities over the years. The 1960s saw the development of a 'school campus' on west side of Preston Road. Firstly, St Joseph's Primary School was opened in 1963 on the site occupied until 1958 by the smelly Gowan Stank Glue Works. The new buildings of Linlithgow Primary School and Linlithgow Academy followed in 1967 and 1968 respectively. Flat roofs were an architectural fashion which

continued on page 88

Left Primary 6 (1999-2000) at St Joseph's Primary School, working hard at their maths.

Opposite New and refurbished housing at Mains Maltings. This complex of buildings started as a distillery founded by William Glen in 1795. By 1854, the distillery had ceased operations, but it was later extended into a brewery maltings which continued until 1968. The remaining mid-19th century buildings, consisting of the three-storey malting barn and store, the flanking square-plan kiln with its pyramidal roof and pagoda ventilator, and the terrace of cottages was converted to housing in 1990-91, at the same time as some new houses were built on the adjacent land.

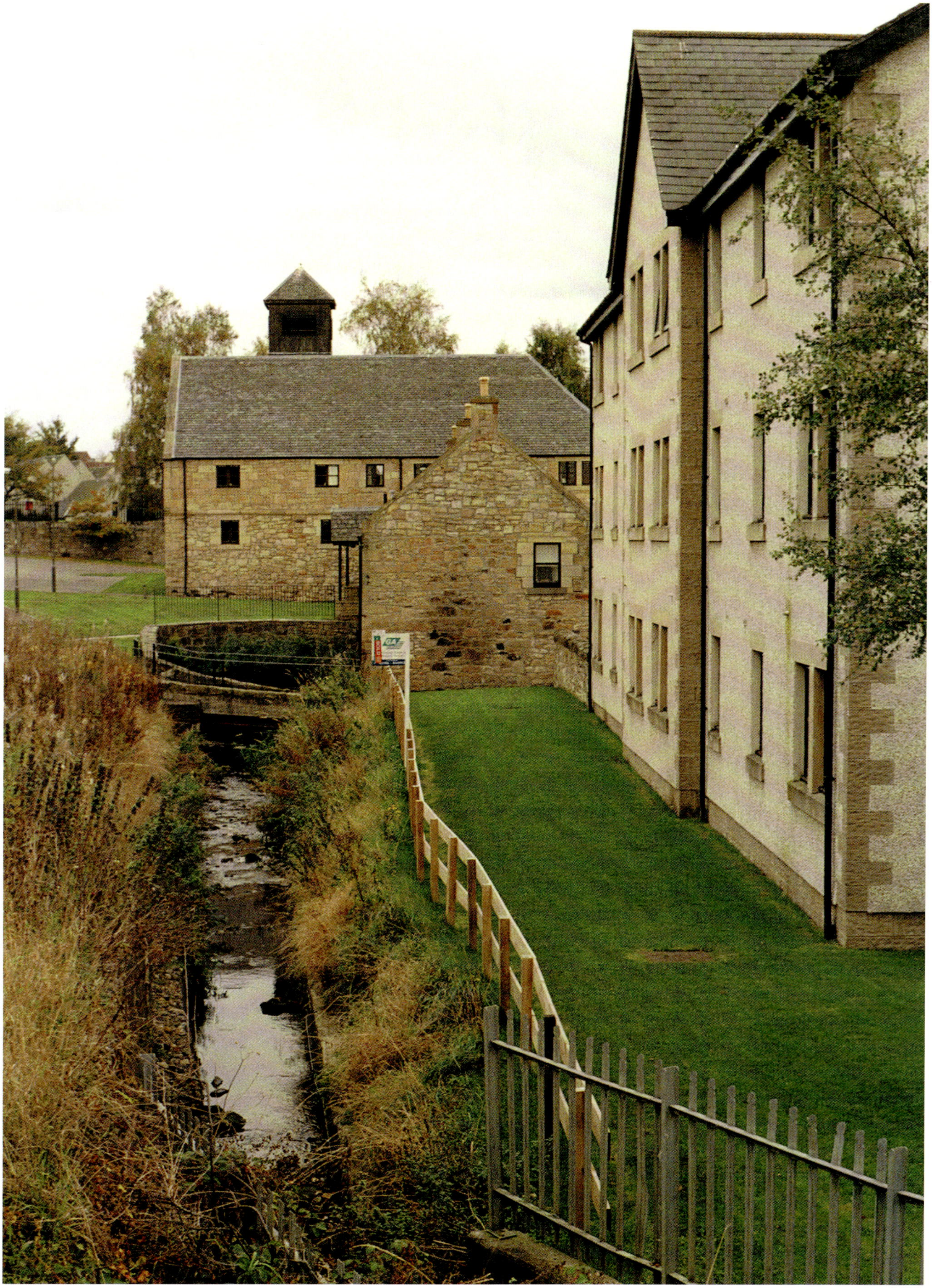

continued from page 86

had to be followed and subsequent maintenance problems were the order of the day! In the field of sport, Linlithgow Golf Club was established in 1913, initially with a nine-hole course. Linlithgow Rose Football Club (winners of the Scottish Junior Cup, for the second time in its history, in 2002!) relocated to Mains Park in 1930, but, at the outbreak of World War II, the ground was sold and converted into a greyhound stadium. The club's present ground at Prestonfield (or, had the club not changed its mind, it could have been called Gowanstank Field) was opened in 1949 and, more recently, Mains Park became the home of Linlithgow Rugby Football Club. The new Linlithgow Leisure Centre has completed the range of major recreational facilities in the area.

Linlithgow Primary School

Linlithgow Primary School in 1999, looking over the playing fields from the south-west. During the headship of William F. Hendrie, the school was particularly noted for media publicity and events, such as 'Primary Press', the award-winning school newspaper, while television cameras recorded events as diverse as a Burns Supper and Glen Michael's Cavalcade.

"Would you like a pizza or a cake?", ask nursery children at Linlithgow Primary School.

The fenced outside area of the nursery at Linlithgow Primary School. Since this photograph was taken in 1999, this scene has completely changed with the demolition of the nursery wing and its replacement with upgraded facilities for the 2002-03 session. These works were undertaken as part of the same Public Private Partnership scheme which included the extension to Low Port Primary School and the new Linlithgow Bridge Primary School. One of the three 'streams' of pupils at Linlithgow Primary School has transferred to the latter, in conjunction with the closure of the West Port Annexe.

Class 7A at Linlithgow Primary School posing for a picture in 1999. Since then, the school has selected a deeper shade of blue for its school uniform which no doubt pleases those who do the laundry!

Two views of the new Linlithgow Leisure Centre, a popular asset to the town, pleasantly located in its green playing field setting. Opened in 1995, the centre includes swimming pool, sports hall, 48-piece 'Techno' gym centre, sauna, steam room, children's soft play area and a cafe, and has an incredible 2,000 members - not bad for a town the size of Linlithgow!

Below Linlithgow Academy, built in 1968 and recently extensively refurbished in an attempt to remedy many of the design faults of the original building. The school is operating at or near capacity (as are all the feeder primary schools in the town) and this has recently been the main reason for refusing permission for additional new housing in Linlithgow. Even so, the Academy is effectively over-subscribed, as pupils from nearby St Joseph's Primary School are routinely refused placing requests.

...flood waters rushed down Golf Course Road

Gable ends to the park at Stewart Avenue. These were the last council houses to be built in Linlithgow, apart from the town centre redevelopment schemes.

The Balfour Beatty private housing development at Kettilstoun Mains. Contrary to best practice elsewhere, West Lothian Council tends to give names to whole developments rather than each street. Thus the cul-de-sac off to the left is denied its individual identity and identified only by the numbers '1-13'. Such culs-de-sac elsewhere in the town do not even have such identification, causing all sorts of problems for delivery drivers and emergency services. Given the wealth of historical associations possessed by the town, and granted that the council consults local experts, how much more interest and variety could be achieved with a bit of imagination! Lennox's Cairn has been relocated very close to the viewpoint of this photograph. This recalls the death of the Earl of Lennox at the Battle of Linlithgow Bridge, fought in 1526.

Later 'executive' housing at Kettilstoun Grove, as seen from the banks of the Union Canal. For no good reason, the road through Kettilstoun Mains changes its name to Kettilstoun Grove and then, due to illogical house numbering, to Kettilstoun Court! Confusion reigns!

This sloping site between the Braehead housing scheme and the Union Canal was owned by the local authority and remained undeveloped for a surprisingly long time. The new houses in the background are a plot development promoted by West Lothian District Council in the mid 1990s, while 25 luxury homes have since been erected in the nearer area by Robertson Residential (Scotland) Ltd. Some Black Bitches thought that perhaps the site might have been better used to accommodate any necessary extensions to the adjacent Linlithgow Academy; however it remains to be seen where the children from all the new houses still being developed will be educated!

The council's plot development at Braehead Park and Golf Course Road, as seen from the banks of the Union Canal, and demonstrating a wide diversity of architectural styles! Not long after the construction of these houses in the mid 1990s, a sudden flash flood caused the Mains Burn to burst its banks. The floodwaters rushed down Golf Course Road and into the Braehead housing scheme, causing considerable damage to property.

The abattoir of R. Y Henderson and Sons Ltd at the corner of Preston Road and Braehead Road. The older part of the slaughterhouse on the left had been established by 1895, but there has been recent talk of relocation to another site at Whitecross, about a mile to the west of Linlithgow Bridge. Although all are agreed that an abattoir is not altogether appropriate for a residential area (nor was the glue works nearby!), the number of houses which the site should accommodate is a burning issue at the time of writing. In the foreground can be seen one set of the 'speed cushions' which, together with more controversial road narrowings elsewhere in Preston Road, are an effective deterrent to 'boy racers' of all ages. It is a pity that all road users have to suffer discomfort because of the irresponsible few!

As can be seen from this plaque on the 1961 road bridge over the River Avon, the main road through Linlithgow (the old A9) was a trunk road funded directly by Central Government, prior to the construction of the M9 motorway.

Linlithgow Bridge

Linlithgow Bridge or 'The Brig' is a community quite distinct from the town of Linlithgow. Prior to the local government reorganisation of 1975, it was administered by West Lothian County Council, rather than Linlithgow Town Council, the responsibilities of which extended only to Stockbridge, and today the village has its own community council. The present bridge over the River Avon replaced a 17th-century structure (1660), built by Alexander, Earl of Linlithgow, who was empowered to charge tolls to compensate for the expenses incurred. The Earl transferred this right to Linlithgow Town Council in 1665 and tolls continued to be collected for another two centuries, until the right was bought out by the county councils of West Lothian and Stirling for the sum of £950. The old bridge was comprehensively repaired in 1810, widened in 1888, and replaced by the present bridge a little to the north in 1961.

The village expanded in association with the establishment of a calico-printing works in 1786, no trace of which survives. The print field on the banks of the River Avon was later occupied by the Avonmill papermill of J Lovell and Sons which, along with the Lochmill Papermill to the north-east of the village, employed a total of 140 people in the mid 1960s. Now both papermills are closed and their sites are occupied by private housing developments of the 1990s - Lovell's Glen (Persimmon Homes) and the east end of Avalon Gardens (Beazer Homes) respectively. Although these mills have disappeared, the Chalmers Hall and the rustic-style cottages on the opposite side of the village Main Street, built for papermill workers, are a lasting reminder of Thomas Chalmers, proprietor at Lochmill.

Other local mills included the Burgh Mill, close to the railway viaduct, which ceased production about 100 years ago and the Little Mill, the remains of which still lie north of the motorway. The latter was the area's last local meal water mill, having existed for over 600 years. Closed on 1 June 1957 on the death of the last miller, Mr J C Fairbairn, it produced animal foodstuffs. Today, Linlithgow Bridge is the location of the area's only industrial estate, at Mill Road.

Opposite Top The Bridge Inn, late 18th century, a popular local hostelry on the other side of the River Avon. Despite being in Stirlingshire, it plays an important part in Linlithgow's Marches Day celebrations.

Opposite Bottom The Chalmers Hall, designed in Arts and Crafts style by the well-known architect, Sir Robert Lorimer, in 1907. The hall is an important asset to the community of Linlithgow Bridge.

Left Chalmers Cottages, attractive housing opposite the hall, by the same architect and of the same date. Originally, the building accommodated seven flats, but the rear stairs to the upper flats have been demolished. The design of identical-looking cottages in Colinton Road, Edinburgh must have been copied for use on this site.

PUBLIC BAR
BAR FOOD &
CHILDRENS MENU
BEER GARDEN
LOUNGE BAR
BAR FOOD
&

F610 SAS
S871 DSG

...costly litigation ended with a House of Lords decision

Another view of the Bridge Inn.

The railway viaduct at Linlithgow Bridge consists of 26 spans, up to 90 feet high. Designed for the Edinburgh and Glasgow Railway by Grainger and Miller engineers, it dates from 1842 and is a scheduled Ancient Monument. Linlithgow Town Council tried to exercise its right to collect tolls for passage over the River Avon by making a claim against the railway company, but prolonged and costly litigation ended with a House of Lords decision in favour of the railway company. The six flat-roofed courtyard houses of 1968 in West View, designed by Lawrence Alexander, are a familiar sight looking down from the viaduct.

Two views of Belsyde Court, the first major private housing development in Linlithgow Bridge, started in the early 1970s by Williamson Homes and completed by Leech Homes (later incorporated into Beazer Homes which has recently been taken over by Persimmon Homes). The range of house-types is limited to three-bedroom semi-detached houses and two-bedroom flats; it is interesting to note that, as elsewhere in the town, there is a fairly rapid turnover of the flats whereas the larger family houses seldom come on to the market. Over the past five years, Beazer Homes has extended the village towards the motorway with its Avalon Gardens development of more upmarket detached houses.

Sainsbury's supermarket under construction in 1999 - within four months of the taking of the photograph, it was open for trading! The finished design at least reflects its location in Scotland rather than the Home Counties and stands out in contrast to the general dereliction of the adjacent prominent sites at the entrance to the town.

The Somerfield supermarket at Stockbridge, built in the early 1990s as a 'Kwiksave' discount store.

Another view of the new Sainsbury's supermarket. In 2002, much of the waste ground in the foreground was the subject of a planning application from Miller Homes for the construction of 23 houses and 12 flats.

Semi-derelict commercial property at Stockbridge. New housing on this site, as proposed by the West Lothian Council, would greatly improve the appearance of Linlithgow's western approach but worsen the town's school capacity and congestion problems.

The new Linlithgow Bridge Primary School under construction, in preparation for its opening in August 2002. The new school has relocated one 'stream' of pupils currently attending Linlithgow Primary School, but controversy has arisen as a result of West Lothian Council's decision to exclude the part of the village south of the Main Street from its catchment area.

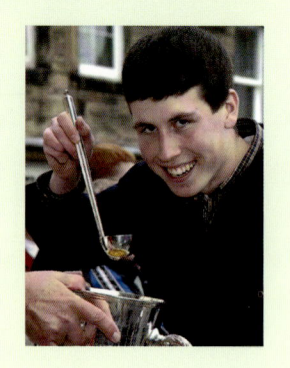

Installation of a deacon at the Cross.

16

Local Customs and Events

The Royal Burgh of Linlithgow has a strong community feeling. Apart from the churches (all mentioned earlier in the text), there are around 80 groups and organisations in the town dependent on volunteers for their operation and survival. The abolition of the Town Council in 1975 dealt a bitter blow to the town, and the continued existence of many of Linlithgow's customs, together with the consideration of local detail, was placed firmly in the hands of the voluntary sector. The Deacons Court was specifically set up in 1974 to replace the Town Council as the organiser of the annual riding of the town's marches or boundaries and other related activities, while the Community Council is heavily involved in arrangements for the Advent Fair. Other important annual events, such as the Children's Gala Day, the Union Canal Rally and the Renaissance Fair, are all put together by enthusiastic committees or groups of individuals.

The Riding of the Marches

Several Scottish burghs, particularly in the Borders, still carry out a ceremonial checking of their ancient 'marches' or boundaries. Linlithgow's Marches celebrations date back at least to the 1389 Royal Burgh charter from Robert II, which granted lands to the town, the boundaries of which had to be upheld. An inspection by foot of the actual boundaries was no doubt originally carried out, but, for many years, the boundary inspections have been limited to the western and eastern extremities, at Linlithgow Bridge and Linlithgow's former seaport of Blackness, respectively. Until the advent of motorised transport, riding on horseback was the order of the day - in previous centuries, up to 300 riders would take part, each trade or fraternity proudly displaying its banner. Marches Day itself is a local public holiday held on the Tuesday in June following the second Thursday. Early warning of the festivities is given the previous Friday by the Town Crier (the 'Crying of the Marches') and, on both the previous Saturdays, Deacons are 'installed' with the aid of the Loving or Waldie cup after processions along the High Street to the Cross.

On Marches Day, the town is roused by flautists, pipers and drummers, then military brass, pipe and reed bands parading around the town from as early as 5am! After 'fraternisation' between the official participants, the Marches procession starts travelling westwards along the High Street to Linlithgow Bridge where toasts are proposed, making further use of the Loving Cup. As well as the marching bands and vehicles carrying the various dignitaries, the highlight is the spectacular array of decorated floats - once their purpose was to show the tools and products of the local trades, now there seems no limit to the range of subject material! Lesser numbers then make their way to Blackness where further refeshments and lunch are consumed. Finally, at 5pm, the main procession is re-assembled at the Low Port and proceeds the traditional three times around the Cross Well, before the final drinking of healths and the singing of 'Auld Lang Syne'.

Left The spectacular 'Peter Pan' float on Marches Day, 1994.

Opposite Another outstanding float at Linlithgow's Riding of the Marches in 1994. Here a mobile version of the United Kingdom's seat of government is seen passing that of the ancient Royal Burgh.

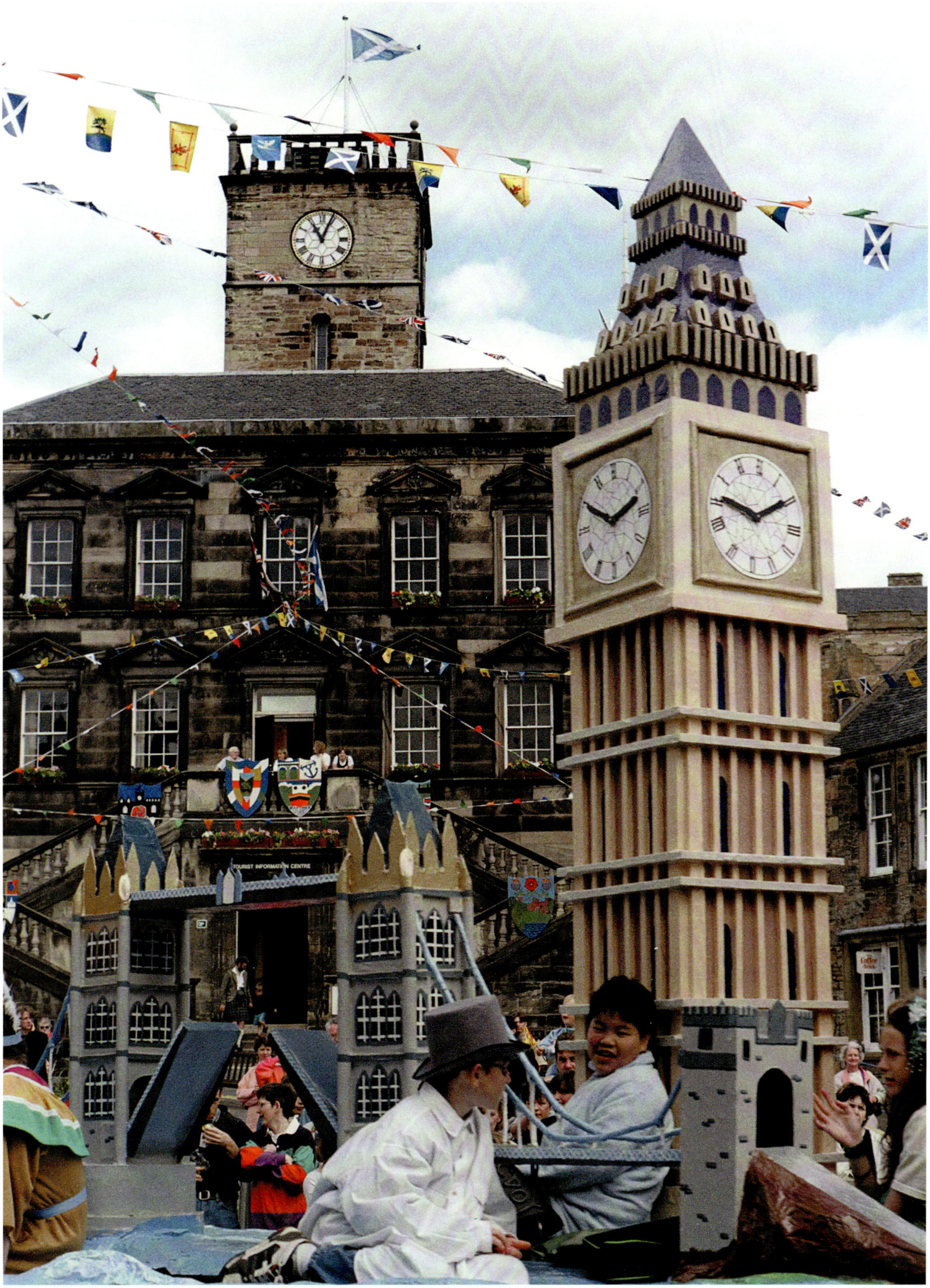

...the highlight, the crowning of the Gala Queen

The crowning of the Linlithgow and Linlithgow Bridge Gala Queen at the Peel, 1991.

Flower girls and fairies parading along the High Street in the 1991 Gala procession.

Bands which normally play at Marches and other local events include the Linlithgow Reed Band (portrayed here at the Peel), the Linlithgow Pipe Band, the Bo'ness and Carriden Band, the Unison Kinneil Silver Band, the Bathgate Band and the West Lothian Samba Band.

The Linlithgow and Linlithgow Bridge Gala Day

Linlithgow has a Children's Gala Day, now normally held on the Saturday following Marches Day. It is kept quite apart from the Marches celebrations, although, to the casual eye, there are strong similarities and links. The Gala Day dates back to 1920 and, since 1930, the highlight has been the crowning of the Gala Queen, a local schoolgirl, in the presence of her attendants - ladies in waiting, bower girls, maids of honour, train bearers, 'Mary Queen of Scots', 'Provost', champion and Scottish soldiers, crown and sceptre bearers, and a large and charming retinue of fairies (Primary 1) and flower girls (Primary 4), all selected by a draw of the names of local school pupils. Participants' houses and gardens are decorated with arches, castles, giant toadstools, bunting, etc. and interested parties tour the town looking for the most impressive and ingenious displays. Gala Day itself starts at Linlithgow Bridge where the participating girls and boys are photographed in all their finery. They then march with another procession of floats and bands to the centre of the town, whence they proceed to the Peel, just to the east of Linlithgow Palace, for the official crowning of the Gala Queen.

View of the festivities from the Manse Road bridge.

Lots of activity in and around the Canal Museum and tearoom, 1999.

The Canal Rally or Annual Fun Day

Every year, on a Sunday in mid-August, the Linlithgow Union Canal Society (LUCS) organises a festive extravaganza in and around the Canal Basin. Boat trips of varying lengths are in continuous operation, and there are stalls (and sometimes children's merry-go-rounds) in the Learmonth Gardens and a varied programme of water-based fun, the highlight of which is the renowned cardboard boat race - a great afternoon out for the family!

The Advent Fair

A more recently-established community event, organised primarily by the town's very active Community Council, is the Advent Fair, held on a Saturday around the beginning of December. During the day, a variety of trading and community activities take place at the Cross and in nearby halls and churches, but the highlight of the proceedings thereafter is a torchlight procession along the High Street from West Port to the Cross, with around 2,500 torch-carrying participants, followed by the singing of Christmas carols, the arrival of Santa Claus and the illumination of the Christmas lights on the town's Christmas tree and elsewhere along the High Street.

Valiant efforts to stay afloat in the cardboard boat race!

99

...a torchlight procession with around 2,500 participants

Linlithgow OLD AND NEW

The impressive Advent torchlight procession wends its way along the High Street.

The Renaissance Festival

The mid-summer Linlithgow Renaissance Festival was first held in 1998. Although it missed a year in 2002, it is intended as an annual celebration of the life and creativity of the town, organised by an association which has drawn support from a wide range of local people and organisations, and aiming to encourage arts of all periods and all forms. Concerts have featured traditional Scottish music and instruments (including the clarsach), Renaissance music and verse, madrigals and minstrels, and ballad singing. There are art exhibitions at the Line Gallery, and activities at other venues have included basketmaking, street games, juggling, talks and a street fair at the Cross. The town also has an annual Folk Festival and a long-established Arts Guild which organises a lively annual programme of musical and dramatic performances.

The Sunday-afternoon Renaissance Fair at the Cross.

Gordon and Liz Beetham appropriately garbed for the Civic Trust's stall at the Renaissance Fair.

References and Photographic Credits

References

BEVERIDGE, James: "Linlithgow at the Scottish Reformation and in the Seventeenth Century", Linlithgow, 1914.
BURROW, Ed J and Co Ltd: "Royal Burgh of Linlithgow – Official Guide", c. 1970
CADELL, Patrick: "Sudden Slaughter: the Murder of the Regent Moray", West Lothian History and Amenity Society, 1975.
CADELL, Patrick (Editor): "The Third Statistical Account of Scotland – The County of West Lothian", Scottish Academic Press, Edinburgh, 1992.
DAWSON OF BONNYTOUN, Adam: "Rambling Recollections of Past Time", Falkirk, 1868.
DENNISON, E. Patricia and COLEMAN, Russel: "Historic Linlithgow", the Scottish Burgh Survey, Historic Scotland, Edinburgh, 2000.
FERGUSON, Rev John: "Linlithgow Palace, its History and Tradition", Edinburgh, 1910.
FERGUSON, Rev John: "Ecclesia Antiqua: the Story of St Michael's Church, Linlithgow", Edinburgh, 1905.
HENDRIE, William: "Images of Scotland – Linlithgow", Tempus Publishing Ltd, Stroud, 1999.
HENDRIE, William: "St Michael's Catholic Church, Linlithgow, 1893-1993", St Michael's RC Church, 1993.
HENDRIE, William: Linlithgow – 600 Years a Royal Burgh", John Donald Publishers Ltd, Edinburgh, 1989.
JAMIESON, Bruce: "Linlithgow in Old Picture Postcards", European Library, Zaltbommel, Netherlands, Second Edition, 1989.
JAMIESON, Bruce: "Old Linlithgow", Stenlake Publishing, Catrine, Ayrshire, 1998.
JAMIESON, Bruce: "The Church of St Michael of Linlithgow", St Michael's Parish Church, c. 1990.
JAQUES, Richard and McKEAN, Charles: "West Lothian – An Illustrated Architectural Guide", The Rutland Press, Edinburgh, 1994.
MACDONALD, Angus: "Linlithgow in Pictures", A and C Black Ltd, London, 1932.
MARTIN, Don and MACLEAN, A A: "Edinburgh and Glasgow Railway Guidebook", Strathkelvin District Libraries, Bishopbriggs, 1992.
McWILLIAM, Colin: "The Buildings of Scotland – Lothian except Edinburgh", Penguin Books Ltd, Harmondsworth, Middlesex, 1978.
POWELL, Mark N: "Linlithgow – A Brief Architectural and Historical Guide, 2nd Edition", Linlithgow Civic Trust, 1990.
RICHARDSON, J S and BEVERIDGE, James: "Linlithgow Palace", Her Majesty's Stationery Office, Edinburgh, 1948.
SCOTTISH EXECUTIVE: Statutory List of Buildings of Architectural/Historic Interest
SIMPSON, Roddy: "Hill and Adamson's Photographs of Linlithgow", West Lothian History and Amenity Society, Linlithgow, 2002.
SKINNER, Basil: "The Union Canal: a Short History of the Edinburgh and Glasgow Union Canal", Linlithgow Union Canal Society, 1977.
SMITH, Alexander: "Dreamthorp: A Book of Essays Written in the Country", London, 1863.
SMITH, Robin: "The Making of Scotland", Canongate Books Ltd, Edinburgh, 2001.
STATISTICAL ACCOUNT: "The Statistical Account of Scotland", 1791-99, edited by J Sinclair. New edition edited by D J Withrington and I R Grant, Wakefield, 1978.
STATISTICAL ACCOUNT: "The New Statistical Account of Scotland", 14 volumes, Edinburgh, 1845.
WALDIE, George: "A History of the Town and Palace of Linlithgow (Third Edition)", G. Waldie, Linlithgow, 1879.

Photographic Credits

All photographs were taken by Christopher Long and Ronald Smith with the exceptions of the following:-

Sarah Ali (page 40, lower).
Staff of Bonnytoun Nursery (page 49, top left).
Christopher Chambers (page 43, lower right).
Margo Crawford (page 46, top left; page 48 (lower); page 49, top right and lower).
Michael Davies (page 77, lower left).
John Dolby (page 21).
Calum Grant (page 23, lower right).
Ross Green (page 86, lower).
Emma Hay (page 38, middle right).
Rowan Jamieson (page 40, top).
Caroline Jess (page 23, middle right)
Pupils of Linlithgow Primary School (page 81, lower right; page 88, all; page 94, lower left).
Linlithgowshire Journal and Gazette (page 96, top; page 100, upper).
May MacGregor (page 80, lower; page 81, top left).
Catherine Joyce McKinlay (page 38, top left; page 53, middle right).
Norma MacLeod (page 59, lower left and lower right; page 64, lower left; page 74, top and lower right; page 75, all)
Euan Marshall (page 42, lower right).
Janette Nixon (page 43, upper and middle right; page 52, middle right; page 99, middle left).
P V Peacock (page 50, middle left and lower left).
Portrait House, Falkirk (page 27).
Stacey Reid (page 77, lower right).
Calum Smith (page 23, lower left; page 24, lower left; page 32, top; page 42, top; page 53, lower right; page 60, middle right; page 64, top).
Myra Smith (page 71, lower left).
Roger Stableford (page 94, middle and lower right); page 95, top right and middle right).
Ian Stirling (page 60, lower left).
Elizabeth Thomson (page 33, top right).
Elisabet Thorin (page 100, both relating to Renaissance Festival).
Tamara Wilson (page 30, lower right; page 67, lower right).

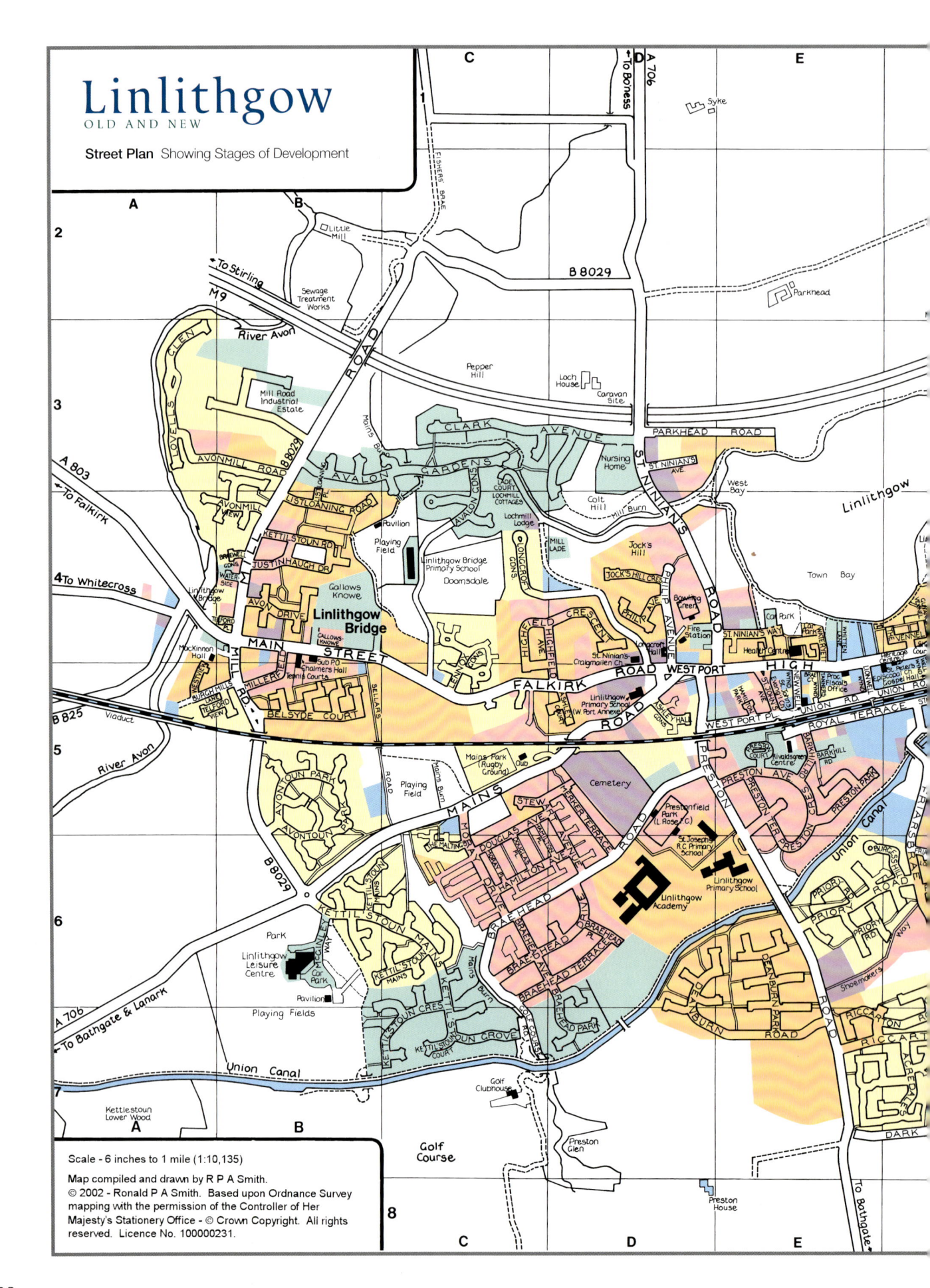

Linlithgow
OLD AND NEW

Street Plan Showing Stages of Development

Scale - 6 inches to 1 mile (1:10,135)

Map compiled and drawn by R P A Smith.
© 2002 - Ronald P A Smith. Based upon Ordnance Survey mapping with the permission of the Controller of Her Majesty's Stationery Office - © Crown Copyright. All rights reserved. Licence No. 100000231.

Periods of Development

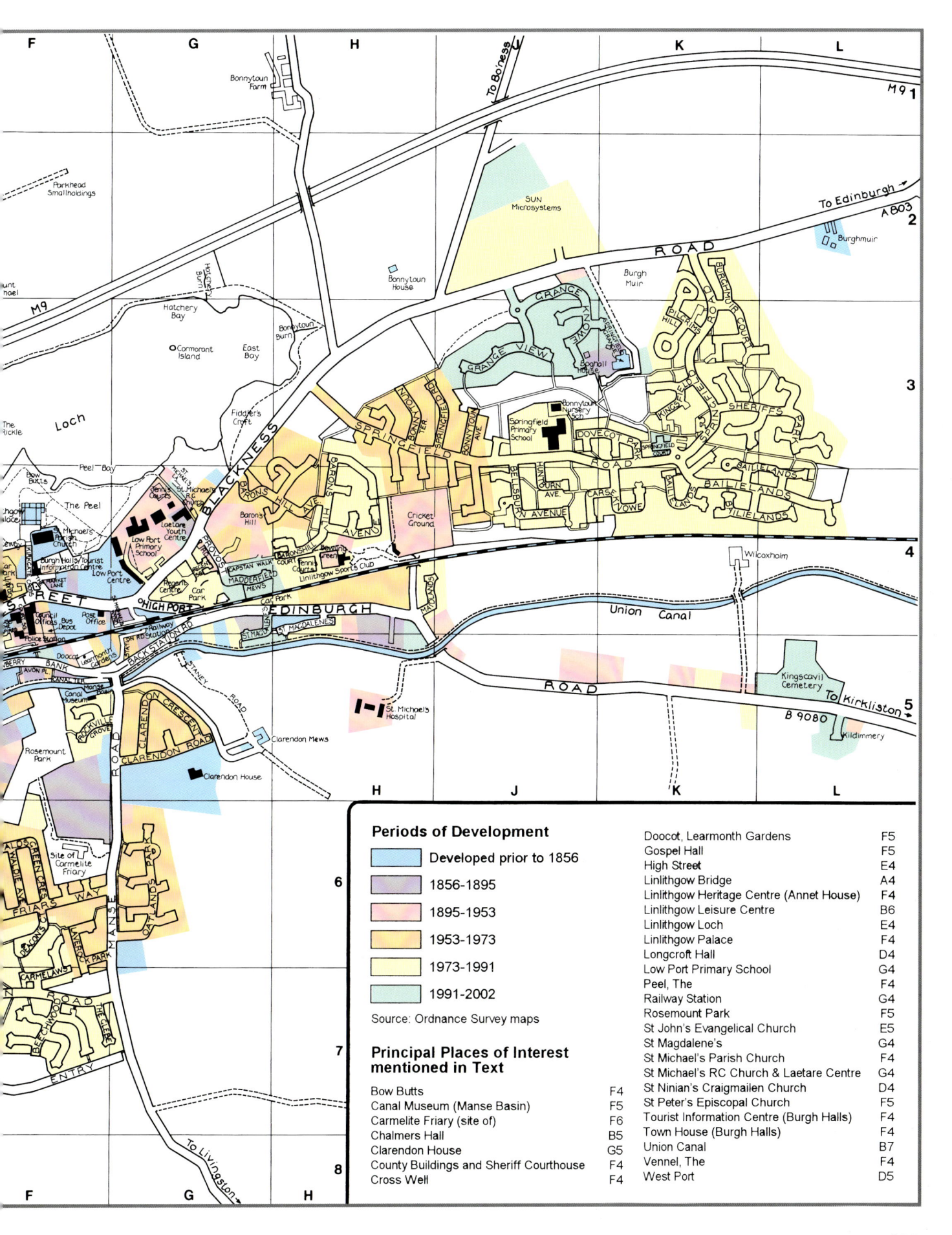

- Developed prior to 1856
- 1856–1895
- 1895–1953
- 1953–1973
- 1973–1991
- 1991–2002

Source: Ordnance Survey maps

Principal Places of Interest mentioned in Text

Bow Butts	F4
Canal Museum (Manse Basin)	F5
Carmelite Friary (site of)	F6
Chalmers Hall	B5
Clarendon House	G5
County Buildings and Sheriff Courthouse	F4
Cross Well	F4
Doocot, Learmonth Gardens	F5
Gospel Hall	F5
High Street	E4
Linlithgow Bridge	A4
Linlithgow Heritage Centre (Annet House)	F4
Linlithgow Leisure Centre	B6
Linlithgow Loch	E4
Linlithgow Palace	F4
Longcroft Hall	D4
Low Port Primary School	G4
Peel, The	F4
Railway Station	G4
Rosemount Park	F5
St John's Evangelical Church	E5
St Magdalene's	G4
St Michael's Parish Church	F4
St Michael's RC Church & Laetare Centre	G4
St Ninian's Craigmailen Church	D4
St Peter's Episcopal Church	F5
Tourist Information Centre (Burgh Halls)	F4
Town House (Burgh Halls)	F4
Union Canal	B7
Vennel, The	F4
West Port	D5

103

Index

abattoir, 91
Advent Fair, 96, 99
Ainslie, John, 17
Airngarth Hill, 55
Alexander, Lawrence, 94
almshouses, 9
Andrew, Provost James, 15
Annet House, 16, 33, 66, 67, 71
Armstrong map, 15
Ashley Hall, 78, 82
Avalon Gardens, 92, 94
Avon Aqueduct, 52
Avonmill papermill, 92
Avontoun Park, 86

Back Station Road, 44, 55
Bailielands, 48
baillies, 7
Baird Hall, 76
Baird, Hugh, 17, 50, 51, 52
Baird, Jessie, 76
Bannockburn, 6
Barbour, John, 6
Barkhill Road, 59
Baron's Hill, 44, 45, 48
Beetham, Gordon & Liz, 100
Beinn Castle Brae, 83
Bell, Rev. Andrew, 16, 18
bells, 26
Bell's Burn, 45
Belsyde Court, 94
Bernham, David de, 5, 26
Black Bitch, 78, 81
Black Death, 7
Blackness, 7, 13, 15, 40
Bo'ness, 7, 14, 15, 17
Bonnie Prince Charlie, 16, 20, 22
Bonnytoun, 46
Bonnytoun House, 47
Bonnytoun Nursery, 49
Bow Butts, 20
Boyd, Provost John, 41
Brae Court, 72
Braehead housing estate, 91
Braehead Park, 52, 91
Braehead Road, 86
Brereton, Sir William, 9
brewing, 17
Brockley's Land, 19
Brown and Wardrop, 33, 76
Brown, Thomas, 31
Bruce, Robert, 6, 22
Bryce, David, 80
Bucknay, Provost John, 16
Bunnock, William, 6
burgh council, 7, 14, 15
Burgh Halls, 8, 30, 31
burgh mills, 9, 92
Burgh Muir, 6, 44
burgh privileges, 7
Burke, William, 17
Burns, Robert, 16, 66

Cadell, William A, 32, 68, 82, 83
Cairns, John, 7
calico, 18, 92
Cambuskenneth Abbey, 5
canal, 17, 47, 50, 52, 60
Canal Basin, 50, 51
Canal House, 50
Canal Museum, 99
Canal Rally, 99
Canal Terrace, 50
Capstan Walk, 45
Carmelite friary, 9, 40, 58, 60
Carnwath, George, 15
castle, 5
Chalmers Cottages, 92
Chalmers, Dr McGregor, 26
Chalmers Hall, 92. 93
Chalmers, Thomas, 80, 92
Chapel of the Blessed Virgin Mary, 8, 9, 40
Charles I, 12, 22
Charter, 7, 96
Christina, Prioress of Manuel, 6
Church, 11
churchyard, 26
Civil War, 11, 12
Clarendon Farm, 61
Clarendon House, 61
Clarendon Road, 56
Clarke, Geoffrey, 26
clock, 31
coats of arms, 4, 39
Coia, J A, 44
Commercial Bank of Scotland, 36
Cornwall of Bonhard, 9, 36
Coulouris, Marie-Louise, 53
County Buildings, 14
Court of the Four Burghs, 7
Court Square, 14
covenanters, 13, 14
craftsmen, 7, 8
crannogs, 20
Crawford of Lochcote, Andrew, 32
cricket, 20, 49
Cromwell, Oliver, 5, 14, 16, 20, 22, 31, 43
Cross, 14, 28, 31, 32, 100

Cross House, 28, 29, 32, 76
Cross Well, 9, 20, 31, 60, 96
Cumberland, Duke of, 16, 22
Cumming, James, 40
Cunzie Neuk, 66
customs, 17, 19

Dalyell of Binns, Thomas, 13
Dark Entry, 56
David I, 5, 22
David II, 7
Dawson of Bonnytoun, Provost Adam, 7, 8, 15, 46, 47
deacons, 7
Deacons Court, 56, 96
Dean of Guild, 8
Deanburn Road, 52, 56
Defoe, Daniel, 15, 17
Dick, George Hay, 83
Dick Peddie & Todd, 33, 71
Dick's Monthly Advertiser, 18, 83
dissenters, 18
distilleries, 17, 44
Dobie, Rev. James, 16
Dog Well Wynd, 11, 68
doocots, 34, 35, 37, 55
Dougal, Jane, 80
Douglas Cottage, 60
Dreamthorp, 19
Drummond of Hawthornden, 9
Drummond of Riccarton, 9, 11
Drury, Sir William, 12
Duncan, John, 74
Dunlop, Agnes, 14

East Port, 40
Edinburgh Road, 44, 46
Edward I, 5, 6, 22
Edward II, 6
Edward III, 6
Elizabeth of Bohemia, 12

factories, 16, 17
Fairbairn, J C, 92
Fairley, J Graham, 42
fairs, 17, 28
falconers, 26
Falkirk Road, 78, 80
Fiddler's Croft, 25
fires, 6, 10, 16, 22, 26, 31, 32, 47
Fleshmarket, 8, 14, 33
Flodden, 10, 26
Folk Festival, 100
Fontane, Theodor, 18
Forrest, Henry, 12, 32
fortifications, 5, 6, 14, 22, 43
Four Marys pub, 14, 34, 38
Frampton, George, 32
French Ambassador's House, 66
French army, 11
French, John, 26
Friars Brae, 56, 60
Friars Way, 60
Friars' Well, 60

gala days, 20, 98
Garner, Robert, 32
George V, 23
Gilmour, Provost Andrew, 19
Glebe House, 61
Glen of Longcroft, Provost James, 19, 32
Glen, Provost Andrew, 14
Glen, William, 86
glue works, 86, 91
Golden Cross Tavern, 62, 66
Golf Course Road, 91
Gordon, Mrs Glen, 16
Gospel Hall, 71
Gowan Stank Glue Works, 86
grammar school, 8, 13, 14, 22, 32
Gray, Robert, 31
Great Inn, 9
'Green Man', 32
Greenyards, 34, 38
Gregory VIII, 5
Guildry House, 8
guilds, 7, 8, 70
Guyancourt Vennel, 62, 63, 64

Hamilton family, 10–13, 17
Hamilton, James, 2nd Earl of Arran, 11
Hamilton, John, Abbot of Arbroath, 11
Hamilton, John, Archbishop of St Andrews, 11, 12, 13
Hamilton of Bothwellhaugh, James, 11–12, 28
Hamilton of Finnart, James, 10
Hamilton of Pardovan, 10, 34
Hamilton of Silvertonhill, James, 10, 83
Hamilton Park, 82
Hamilton, Patrick, 12–13, 32
Hamilton, Thomas, 14
Hamilton's Land, 34, 35, 37
Hamiltons of Kingscavil, 9
Hamiltons of Pardovan, 9
Hamiltons of Westport, 9, 17
Hare, William, 17
Hawley, General, 16
health centre, 72, 75, 77

hearth tax, 15
Hendrie, W F, 65, 88
Henry VIII, 10, 11
Herriot, Alan, 71
High Port, 8, 40
High Street, 5, 8, 9, 15, 19, 34
Highfield, 78
Hill, Amelia, 28
Hill, David O, 18
Holmes Partnership, 47
Holyrood Abbey, 9
Honeyman and Keppie, 26
Hope, Adrian, 55
horse market, 81
housing, 8, 16, 18, 19
Hurd (Robert) and Partners, 40

Jacobites, 16
Jacques, Richard, 65
James I, 10, 22
James II, 10
James IV, 10, 26
James V, 10, 20, 22, 26
James VI, 11, 12, 22
Jamieson, Bruce, 28

Katie Wearie's Tree, 81
Kettilstoun, 5
Kettilstoun Court, 90
Kettilstoun Grove, 90
Kettilstoun Mains, 90
Kettilstoun Road, 82
Kirkgate, 5, 8, 14, 28, 29, 30
Kirkwood, James, 14, 15, 19
Knights of St John, 6, 9, 39
Knox, John, 12

Laetare Centre, 44
landowners, 17
Langside, Battle of, 11, 15
Laverock Park, 56
Learmonth Gardens, 55
Learmonth, Provost Alexander, 55
leather, 16, 70, 75, 77
leisure centre, 88, 89
Lennox Gardens, 78
Lennox, John Stewart, 3rd Earl of, 10, 90
Lennox 's Cairn, 10, 90
leper house, 9
Lindisfarne, 77
Lindsay, Sir David, 10
linen, 15, 17
Linlithgow Academy, 42, 81, 86, 89, 91
Linlithgow, Alexander, Earl of, 92
Linlithgow and Stirlingshire Hunt, 41
Linlithgow Boll, 7
Linlithgow Bridge, 92–95
Linlithgow Bridge, Battle of, 10, 90
Linlithgow Bridge Primary School, 88, 91
Linlithgow, Earls of, 9, 12, 14, 15
Linlithgow East United Presbyterian Church, 55
Linlithgow Free Church, 80
Linlithgow Gazette, 33
Linlithgow, George, 3rd Earl, 14, 15
Linlithgow Heritage Trust, 71
Linlithgow, John Hope, 7th Earl of Hopetoun, Marquess of, 32
Linlithgow Primary School, 81, 86, 88
Linlithgow West United Presbyterian Church, 68, 77
Lion Chamber, 23
Lion Well Wynd, 68, 72, 74
Little Mill, 92
Livingston, Archibald of, 6
Livingston family, 14–15
Loch, 20, 24, 25
Lochmill papermill, 19, 80, 92
Longcroft Hall, 42, 81
Longcroft House, 80
Lorimer, Sir Robert, 92
Lovell's Glen, 9
Loving Cup, 38, 96
Low Port, 8, 9, 40
Low Port Centre, 40, 45
Low Port Hut, 43
Low Port Primary School, 41, 42, 43, 45, 55
Luband, Piers de, 6
LUCS, 18, 51, 52, 99

McCartney, N Crear, 26
McGinley, Jimmy, 67
McGovern, Father, 44
McGowran, Tom, 71
McKean, Charles, 65
McWilliam, Colin, 28
Madderfield Mews, 45
Maidlands, 46
Mains Burn, 91
Mains Maltings, 86
Mains Park, 88
Malcolm IV, 5
Manse Road, 50, 61
Manuel, 6, 9
map, 102
Mar, John de, 6
Marches, 28, 53, 92, 95, 96, 97

Mary of Guise, 10, 11
Mary, Queen of Scots, 10–11, 15, 22, 26, 66, 71, 98
Masonic Lodge, 33, 66
Mercat Cross, 8, 28
Mickel, Robert, 80
Middle Raw, 8, 9
Millar, William, 61
Millennium Link, 51
Miller, John, 53
Milne, Provost Alexander, 15
Milne, Robert, 14
Mint, 9, 34, 39
Moncrieff, George, 17
Montrose, James Graham, Marquis of, 13
Moray, James Stewart, Earl of, 11–12, 28
Morrison, Margaret, 75
Morrison Shoe Shop, 75
Murray, Lord George, 16
Mylne, John, 31

National Covenant, 13, 14
National Trust, 34
Nether Parkley, 61
New Statistical Account, 18, 31
New Well, 72
New Well Wynd, 72
Newlands (Alexander) & Sons, 46
Nobel, Alfred, 40

Oatlands Park, 56
Old Statistical Account, 15, 16–17

Palace, 5, 8, 10, 12, 14, 16, 20, 22, 24, 25
Palace Gateway, 20, 30
Palace Hotel, 37
Palace Well, 20
papermills, 19, 80, 92
Parr Partnership, 47
Paterson, Rev Ian, 26
Paton, Sir Noel, 28
Paul's Well, 81
Peel, 6, 7, 20
Philip Avenue, 78
Philiphaugh, Battle of, 13
pigeon lofts, 34, 35, 37
Pilgrim's Hill, 45
Pinker, R Hope, 38
plagues, 7
police station, 33
Pollock, Thom, 83
Pont, Timothy, 8
population, 4, 18
ports, 8, 40, 78
Post Office, 38
Preston Court, 59
Preston Park, 82
Preston Road, 51, 56, 59, 82, 84, 86, 91
Priory Road, 56
prison, 18, 31, 33
Provost Road, 45
provosts, 7, 14, 15, 16, 19, 32, 41, 47, 98
Provost's lamp, 33
public library, 62, 63, 67, 71
pubs, 33, 34, 38, 70, 72, 73, 81, 92, 93, 94
Pugin and Pugin, 44

Queen Elizabeth II, 23, 26, 51
Queen Margaret's Bower, 10
Queen Victoria, 26

Racal, 56
Raebuck, John, 6
railway, 17, 18, 50
railway station, 50, 53
Ratho, 17
Red Lion, 9
Reformation, 11, 12–13, 26
Regent Centre, 40
Regent Square, 50
Regent Works, 19, 40
Renaissance Festival, 100
Rennie, John, 17
Restoration, 14, 20
Rhind, David, 56
Riccarton Road, 56
Richard, J Miller, 61
riggs, 8, 34, 50, 71
riots, 15
Ritchie, John, 31
Rivaldsgreen Centre, 59
Rivaldsgreen House, 60, 80
Rivaldsgreen tan works, 59
Rivaldsgreen water works, 59
RMJM, 43
Robert II, 7, 96
Rockville, 61
Rohan, Henri, Duc de, 12
Rosemount House, 61
Rosemount Park, 25, 31, 60, 61
Ross of Halkhead, 9, 15, 55
Rowand Anderson, Kininmonth and Paul, 31, 64, 72
Royal Bank of Scotland, 36
Royal Terrace, 56, 57, 58

St Andrews Priory, 5
St George, James de, 6, 22

St John's Avenue, 83
St John's Evangelical Church, 72
St Joseph's Primary School, 44, 76, 86, 89
St Magdalene's, 16
St Magdalene's Distillery, 44, 45, 46
St Magdalene's Hospital, 40, 46
St Michael's Church, 9, 10, 11, 20, 22, 24, 26, 28, 30
St Michael's Hospital, 46
St Michael's RC Church, 44, 76
St Michael's Well, 39
St Michael's Wynd, 39, 50
St Ninian's Chapel, 8, 9, 40, 78, 80
St Ninian's Craigmailen Church, 68, 80, 81, 84
St Ninian's Way, 77, 85
St Peter's Convent, 44
St Peter's Episcopal Church, 71
Satire of the Three Estates, 10
schools, 6, 13, 14, 22, 32, 41, 42, 43, 45, 60, 78, 81, 86, 88, 95
Scott, William, 31, 33, 40, 45, 84
seal, 4
sheriff court, 28, 31, 33
Sheriffmuir, Battle of, 15
Sheriff's Park, 48
shoemakers, 16, 70, 75
Shoemakers' Land, 70
Shoemakers Way, 61
Skeoch, David, 14
Slezer, John, 8, 9, 14
Smith, Alexander, 16, 19
Smith, George, 74
Smith, John, 31
Somerville, Gordon Duncan, 50
South Vennel, 8
Spanish Ambassador's House, 19, 66
sports clubs, 49, 88
Springfield housing estate, 44, 47, 48, 49
Star and Garter, 41
Station Road, 55
Steel, Dr David, 26
Stewart Avenue, 90
Stockbridge, 95
Strawberry Bank, 58
Stuart, Charles Edward, 16, 20, 22
Stuart House, 72
Sun Microsystems, 19, 44, 47
supermarkets, 40, 95
Swan Tavern, 72, 73
swans, 20

tanneries, 77
teinds, 5, 9, 58
Telford, Thomas, 17, 52
Temple lands, 9
Third Statistical Account, 19
Todd, Walter, 33
tolbooth, 8, 14, 22
tombstones, 20
town wall, 8
trade, 4, 7, 15
Tudor, Margaret, 10, 26

Union Canal, 17, 47, 50, 52, 60
Union Road, 58, 59, 68, 71
United Presbyterian Church, 80

Vennel development, 36, 62, 64, 65, 66, 67
viaduct, 94
Victoria Halls, 19, 37

wages, 16
Waldie, David, 19, 34, 38
Walker, J Russell, 37
Wallace, William, 6
Walpole, G H S, 71
war memorial, 26
Wardrop & Reid, 61
Wars of Independence, 6–7
Water Yett, 72
Watergate, 62
Wellbank, 55
West Port, 8, 78, 80, 81, 82
West Port Annexe, 81, 88
West Port flats, 43
West Port House, 78, 83
West View, 94
Wheeler and Sproson, 40
Whitten Fountain, 41
Whitworth, Robert, 17
wildlife, 20
William the Lion, 5
Winchburgh, 17
Winzet, Ninian, 13
witchcraft, 13–14
women workers, 18
Wood's map, 38, 41
workhouse, 46
wynds, 9, 11, 34, 39, 50, 68, 72, 74
Wyville Thomson, Charles, 19

yard-heads, 8